101 BIBLE WORD SEARCHES

VOLUME 1

Puzzles Created by
Angela Fletcher
Ruth Graether
N. Teri Grottke
Conover Swofford

BARBOUR
PUBLISHING

© 2006 by Barbour Publishing, Inc.

Project Manager: Connie Troyer. Additional editorial assistance by
Donna Maltese.

ISBN 978-1-59789-474-6

All scripture quotations are taken from the King James Version of the
Bible.

Published by Barbour Publishing, Inc., P.O. Box 719, Uhrichsville,
Ohio 44683.

*Our mission is to publish and distribute inspirational products offering
exceptional value and biblical encouragement to the masses.*

 Member of the
Evangelical Christian
Publishers Association

Printed in the United States of America.

Welcome to

101 Bible Word Searches!

If you like Bible word searches, you'll love this book. Here are 101 brand-new puzzles to expand your Bible knowledge and test your word search skills, as thousands of search words await your discovery—each one based on or directly selected from the King James Version of the Bible. You're in for hours of fun!

101 Bible Word Searches contains two types of puzzles. You'll find traditional word search lists, with 22–35 entries based on a common theme, as well as scripture passages with the search words printed in **bold type**. When a phrase in a scripture passage is **bold and underlined**, those words will be found together in the puzzle grid. Occasionally, only part of a word in a scripture passage puzzle will need to be located; in that case, only the part to be found is in **bold**. When a word list phrase including [brackets] is used, the words within brackets will not be in the puzzle. If you get stuck, answers are provided at the back of the book.

We know you're eager to get started, so our final word is this: Enjoy!

1

Biblical Alphabet

ARMAGEDDON
BUTLER
COUNTENANCE
DAMASCUS
EASTWARD
FATHER
GENTLENESS
HYPOCRITES
INIQUITY
JAVELIN
KINSWOMAN
LANGUAGE
MONEYCHANGERS

NATIVITY
OMNIPOTENT
PESTILENCE
QUIVERED
RESURRECTION
SYNAGOGUE
THANKSGIVING
UNDERSTANDING
VASHTI
WISDOM
YESTERDAY
ZEALOUSLY

```
V A R S T N A M O W S N I K A S
S H E R E H T A F Z Q U Q R L S
G T S E A S T W A R D U M A R E
N E U G O G A N Y S I A N E E N
I I R N I T H S A V G G L S C E
D E R A Z S R Q E E U T W E N L
N Y E H W I W R D A U Q I T E T
A E C C M W E D G B X X S I L N
T S T Y R D O E Y Z Y Z D R I E
S T I E C N A N E T N U O C T G
R E O N T N E T O P I N M O S Z
E R N O H H N I L E V A J P E X
D D A M A S C U S H H S R Y P Y
N A H G N I V I G S K N A H T M
U Y L S U O L A E Z Z Z X L I W
I N I Q U I T Y T I V I T A N X
```

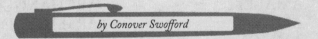

by Conover Swofford

2

A's in the Bible

AARON
ABADDON
ABBA
ABEL
ABSALOM
ACCURSED
ACTS
ALEXANDER
ALPHA
ALTAR
AMALEK
AMEN
AMMON
AMOS

ANANIAS
ANCIENT OF
  DAYS
ANDREW
ANGEL
ANOINT
ANTICHRIST
ANTIOCH
APOLLOS
AQUILA
ARCHANGEL
ARMAGEDDON
ASSYRIA

A	A	M	M	N	N	R	E	D	N	A	X	E	L	A
H	A	B	A	B	S	A	L	O	M	A	A	M	M	M
S	T	C	A	A	A	N	T	I	C	H	R	I	S	T
Y	R	A	A	R	M	A	G	E	D	D	O	N	T	B
A	L	P	H	A	E	L	S	O	M	A	M	E	N	L
D	N	N	A	N	H	E	M	M	M	O	A	M	I	E
F	N	O	C	N	T	G	D	A	L	T	A	R	O	G
O	H	D	C	D	A	N	D	A	A	A	M	M	N	N
T	C	D	U	A	N	A	S	A	I	N	A	N	A	A
N	O	A	R	M	A	M	M	O	N	D	A	P	A	H
E	I	B	S	A	A	Q	U	I	L	A	O	A	D	C
I	T	A	E	L	A	A	M	M	H	L	R	D	D	R
C	N	D	D	E	A	A	M	C	L	O	A	B	B	A
N	A	D	C	K	C	C	A	O	N	C	A	B	E	L
A	S	S	Y	R	I	A	S	A	W	E	R	D	N	A

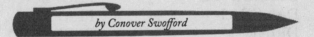

by Conover Swofford

⚡Bonus Trivia

What famed evangelist was intentionally
not named for his priestly father?

John the Baptist. (Luke 1:57–60)

3

Aaron's Golden Calf

Exodus 32

AARON
ALTAR
BRAKE
BREAK
BURNT
OFFERINGS
CONSECRATE
CORRUPTED
DANCING
DRINK
EARRINGS
EGYPT
FEAST
FIRE
FORGIVE
GAVE
GODS
GOLD

GRAVING TOOL
HAND
ISRAEL
LAND
LORD
MOSES
PEACE
PEOPLE
PLAY
REPENTED
SACRIFICED
SEED
SELF
SIN
STARS
WAR
WRATH

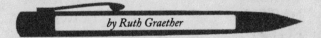
by Ruth Graether

```
D R M O D W E S D N C W S G S
Q A S O R N O G L S O W A R G
E D N A S F K N O T N R F B N
K K T C C E I I G A S L A C I
A H N M I R S R V R E N O A R
R D V I A N I E E S C R L F R
B T R T R E G F I G R V A O A
G S L O X D I F I U A O L R E
A A Z Y L V P O P C T M T G G
V E R E P E N T E D E S T I O
E F H Z O P E N S I N D E V D
E G Y P T D P R P E A C E E S
J P L A Y K U U K A E R B B D
M E D N A H Y B L E A R S I A
G R A V I N G T O O L D N A L
```

⚡Bonus Trivia

What did Jesus say God would do for the believers He sees secretly giving to the needy?

Reward them openly. (Matthew 6:3–4)

4

The Call and Blessing of Abram

Genesis 12; 14:18–19

ABRAM
ALTAR
BETHEL
BLESSING
CANAAN
COUNTRY
CURSE
EARTH
EGYPT
FAMINE
GOD
GREAT
HARAN
HOUSE
JOURNEYED

KINDRED
LAND
LORD
LOT
NAME
NATION
PHARAOH
PLAGUED
SARAI
SEED
SHEEP
SICHEM
SISTER
SOJOURN
WIFE

by Ruth Graether

```
S S F L O D C T D A L X Q N A
E Y I H O U S E A O E D A G B
U G A C S R Y L T U N T W R E
K E Y A H E D P P A I E I E T
O I R P N E K H L O M L F A H
H A N R T E M A N P A O E T E
I T U D O G X R L V F U F E L
E O R X R R G A N R U O J O S
J S M A E E G O Y M A R B A N
D C R T E U D H O R N A M E A
E K S U E P E E H S T Y Q R R
E I H D C B E K T R J N A Q A
S R B L E S S I N G G T U V H
C A N A A N V Q C N L Q Y O H
U M O C R X K U L A S B M E C
```

⚡Bonus Trivia

What language phenomenon happened to people from many nations gathered at Pentecost?

Each heard the gospel in his own language. (Acts 2:1–11)

5

People in the Book of Acts

AENEAS
CHIEF CAPTAIN
CORNELIUS
CRISPUS
DEMETRIUS
ELYMAS
GAMALIEL
HOLY GHOST
JAMES
JASON
JESUS
JOHN
JUSTUS
LAME

LUCIUS
MNASON
PAUL
PETER
PHILIP
PHILOSOPHERS
RHODA
SCEVA
SERGIUS PAULUS
SEVEN SONS
SIMEON
SIMON
SORCERY
TROPHIMUS

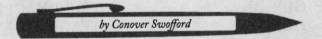

by Conover Swofford

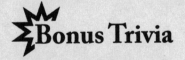

Bonus Trivia

Which four men became fairer in
countenance through a vegetarian diet?

Daniel, Hananiah, Mishael, and Azariah. (Daniel 1:11–15)

6

Places Where Altars Were Built

ARARAT
ATHENS
BEERSHEBA
BETHEL
CANAAN
CARMEL
DAMASCUS
EBAL
GIBEON
HEBRON
JERUSALEM

JORDAN
MIZPEH
MORIAH
RAMAH
REPHIDIM
SAMARIA
SHECHEM
SINAI
TABERNACLE
TEMPLE
ZOPHIM

```
B D L E I F J M W V S B M M Z
E H X O F X J E O H V T I E O
E B A W G I G A R R Y O Z H P
R B E M W S T T I U I A P C H
S G Y Y A H A A F B S A E E I
H T A B E R N A C L E A H H M
E N Q N A I U D B W M X L S F
B A S R S I A M I D I H P E R
A D A I N M R C A R M E L E M
R R Q L A O O A J H M C L D Z
E O Y S N Q E M M P E P U H B
K J C E B A L B K A M B R T Q
K U H K I N W H I E S O R Z Z
S B E T H E L W T G N H U O M
L S N A A N A C G E U X D P N
```

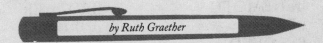

by Ruth Graether

⚡Bonus Trivia

What three gifts did the wise men bring
to the infant Jesus?

7

B's in the Bible

BABEL	BIRTH
BAKER	BISHOP
BALAAM	BLESSED
BAPTIZE	BLIND
BARABBAS	BLOOD
BARNABAS	BOOK OF LIFE
BARUCH	BOOTHS
BATHSHEBA	BRASEN
BEGINNING	BREAD
BEGOTTEN	BROOD
BEHEMOTH	BROTHER
BELIAL	BURDEN
BELOVED	BURIAL
BETHLEHEM	BUTLER

```
B A R A B B A S E Z I T P A B
B B B R A H T O M E H E B I B
B R R B B L E S S E D C S D B
B N M B B E L O V E D H B A R
E L E M B E H E M O O M K B O
G F I D Z A T T A P O E R R T
O X I N R T R H A X R S S S H
T D D L D U I N L X B R S C E
T M D R F L B B A E B B U B R
E B A B A O R R B B H R B L S
N K E I K H K H H A A E B O S
Z Z R X S H T O O B B S M O S
Y U B R A S E N O M B B M D S
B G N I N N I G E B U T L E R
L A I L E B A B E H S H T A B
```

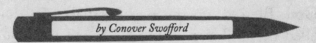

by Conover Swofford

8

The Beatitudes

Matthew 5:3–12

Blessed are the **poor** in **spirit**: for theirs is the **kingdom** of **heaven**. Blessed are they that **mourn**: for they shall be **comforted**. Blessed are the **meek**: for they shall **inherit** the **earth**. Blessed are they which do **hunger** and **thirst** after righteousness: for they shall be filled. Blessed are the **merciful**: for they shall obtain mercy. Blessed are the **pure** in **heart**: for they shall see **God**. Blessed are the **peacemakers**: for they shall be called the **children** of God. Blessed are they which are **persecuted** for **righteousness**' sake: for theirs is the kingdom of heaven. Blessed are ye, when **men** shall **revile** you, and persecute you, and shall say all **manner** of **evil** against you **falsely,** for my sake. **Rejoice**, and be **exceeding glad**: for great is your **reward** in heaven: for so persecuted they the **prophets** which were before you.

```
T H M M I R H T T T S R I H T
F M R H U N G E R N E V A E H
A E R U P E A C E M A K E R S
L R G N I D E E C X E I L E S
S C O M H E E S E X E N I W E
E I D E X X T S D A L G V A N
L F X L M E X C S M X D E R S
Y U H C H I L D R E N O R D U
R L H P T R M L S E L M H T O
O O O R T H I L L K L B X C E
O R A E E V X C I N H E R I T
P E R S E C U T E D E A R T H
H O H R H D E T R O F M O C G
O F C R E N N A M O U R N J I
T O S P I R I T E C I O J E R
```

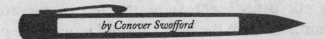

by Conover Swofford

⚡Bonus Trivia

Where was the young Jesus found when
He was missing for three days after
the Feast of the Passover?

In the temple. (Luke 2:41–46)

9

Balaam's First Prophecy

Numbers 23:7–10

And he took up his **parable**, and said, **Balak** the king of **Moab** hath brought me from **Aram**, out of the **mountains** of the **east**, saying, Come, **curse** me **Jacob**, and come, defy **Israel**. How shall I curse, whom **God** hath not cursed? or how shall I defy, whom the LORD hath not defied? For from the top of the **rocks** I see him, and from the **hills** I **behold** him: lo, the **people** shall **dwell** alone, and shall not be **reckoned** among the **nations**. Who can **count** the **dust** of Jacob, and the number of **the fourth** part of Israel? Let me die the **death** of the **righteous**, and let my last **end** be like **his**!

```
P A R A B L E R B P E O P L E
C D H I S E F I D G O D G H L
L O R D G J K G L L R N U P M
Q T R S N T U H O C O U N T O
V H K X I L Z T H R T C Q E U
B E F G L H I E E C K B L V N
A F H I L L S O B N M O A B T
L O N O E P Q U R A S C T U A
A U V W W X E S Y T Z A A E I
K R B O D S D I F I G J K N N
I T J K R L M N S O B P Q D S
D H S U R E C K O N E D G T U
U V C W X Y C Z I S R A E L A
S B C D E O F H T A E D G H I
T J K A R A M L V N X E A S T
```

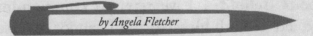

by Angela Fletcher

⚡ Bonus Trivia

Which four little creatures are said to be
exceedingly wise?

Ants, conies, locusts, and spiders. (Proverbs 30:24–28)

10

Balaam's Second Prophecy

Numbers 23:18–24

And he took up his parable, and said, **Rise** up, Balak, and **hear**; hearken unto me, thou son of **Zippor**: **God** is not a **man**, that he should **lie**; neither the son of man, that he should **repent**: hath he **said**, and shall he not **do** it? or hath he **spoken**, and shall he not make it good? **Behold**, I have received **commandment** to bless: and he hath **blessed**; and I cannot **reverse** it. He hath not beheld **iniquity** in **Jacob**, neither hath he seen **perverseness** in **Israel**: the LORD his God is with him, and the shout of a **king** is among them. God brought them out of **Egypt**; he hath as it were the strength of an **unicorn**. Surely there is no **enchantment** against Jacob, neither is there any **divination** against Israel: according to this time it shall be said of Jacob and of Israel, What hath God wrought! Behold, the people shall rise up as a <u>**great lion**</u>, and lift up himself as a <u>**young lion**</u>: he shall not lie **down** until he eat of the **prey**, and drink the blood of the slain.

N	R	I	S	E	C	J	K	U	E	G	Y	P	T	E
E	N	C	H	A	N	T	M	E	N	T	C	G	O	D
O	D	O	P	R	E	P	E	N	T	E	O	H	I	C
D	J	A	C	O	B	P	L	T	V	D	M	N	O	S
C	E	I	Q	B	D	R	D	S	K	L	M	O	N	S
Z	F	S	R	A	E	E	M	R	W	N	A	I	U	E
I	S	R	S	Z	S	Y	M	A	X	O	N	L	V	N
P	A	A	T	S	P	O	K	E	N	I	D	T	L	E
P	I	E	E	Y	F	I	N	Q	Y	L	M	A	O	S
O	D	L	U	X	D	O	W	N	Z	G	E	E	R	R
R	B	Y	T	I	U	Q	I	N	I	N	N	R	D	E
G	N	I	K	N	R	O	C	I	N	U	T	G	W	V
A	L	E	V	W	G	H	B	E	H	O	L	D	X	R
D	I	V	I	N	A	T	I	O	N	Y	P	Q	Y	E
L	M	R	E	V	E	R	S	E	B	H	E	A	R	P

by Angela Fletcher

⚡Bonus Trivia

What did Saul do when a light from heaven flashed around him?

He fell to the earth. (Acts 9:3–4)

11

Balaam's Third Prophecy

Numbers 24:3–9

And he took up his parable, and said, **Balaam** the son of **Beor** hath said, and the man whose **eyes** are **open** hath said: He hath said, which heard the words of **God**, which saw the **vision** of the **Almighty, falling** into a trance, but having his eyes open: How goodly are thy **tents**, O Jacob, and thy **tabernacles**, O Israel! As the **valleys** are they **spread** forth, as **gardens** by the <u>river's side</u>, as the trees of lign **aloes** which the LORD hath planted, and as **cedar trees** beside the **waters**. He shall **pour** the water out of his buckets, and his **seed** shall be in many waters, and his king shall be higher than **Agag**, and his **kingdom** shall be **exalted**. God brought him forth out of Egypt; he hath as it were the **strength** of an unicorn: he shall eat up the nations his enemies, and shall break their bones, and **pierce** them through with his **arrows**. He couched, he lay down as a **lion**, and as a great lion: who shall stir him up? Blessed is he that blesseth thee, and cursed is he that curseth thee.

```
A B E O R B C D S E G O D F G
A N M L E X A L T E D K H I H
O L P G A R D E N S Q D T R S
E C O B A Z Y S E E R T G U T
Y D D E E A F G T O L H N I O
E P E O S N L M L L I K E R P
S C E D A R Q M T U O V R I E
W Q S R S V I S I O N S T V N
O X Y P O U R Z A G B R S E E
B V A L L E Y S E S H E C R D
F K I N G D O M W H I T J S A
F A L L I N G O N N M A Y S E
O P A G A G R R S T U W V I R
B T A B E R N A C L E S Y D P
C B A L A A M D P I E R C E S
```

by Angela Fletcher

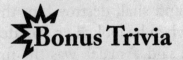

Bonus Trivia

How did Ruth show her interest in Boaz
at the threshing floor?

She lay at his feet. (Ruth 3:2–5)

12

Balaam's Fourth Prophecy

Numbers 24:15–24

And he took up his parable, and said, Balaam the **son** of Beor hath said, and the **man** whose eyes are open hath said: He hath said, which heard the words of **God**, and knew the knowledge of the **most High**, which **saw** the **vision** of the **Almighty**, **falling** into a trance, but having his eyes open: I shall see **him**, but not now: I shall **behold** him, but not nigh: there shall come a **Star** out of **Jacob**, and a **Sceptre** shall **rise** out of Israel, and shall **smite** the corners of **Moab**, and **destroy** all the **children** of Sheth. And **Edom** shall be a possession, **Seir** also shall be a possession for his enemies; and Israel shall do valiantly. Out of Jacob shall come he that shall have **dominion**, and shall destroy him that remaineth of the city. And when he looked on **Amalek**, he took up his parable, and said, Amalek was the first of the nations; but his latter end shall be that he perish for ever. And he looked on the **Kenites**, and took up his parable, and said, Strong is thy dwellingplace, and thou puttest thy nest in a rock. Nevertheless the Kenite shall be wasted, until Asshur shall carry thee away captive. And he took up his parable, and said, Alas, who shall live when God doeth this! And ships shall come from the coast of **Chittim**, and shall afflict Asshur, and shall afflict **Eber**, and he also shall perish for ever.

```
S O N E F X Y B E H O L D A X
A Q G D E S T R O Y W A C V C
W S O T S W Z M A R X L H U Z
C A D W G V R L M I S M I T A
D O S O H U E K A S E I T K M
H N C G M T B E L E T G T R A
G M E N I I E J E V I H I E N
I D P I C N N I K S N T M P B
H K T L I S R I N N E Y H O C
T P R L K R A H O U K F M N F
S I E A L Q T I O N P E O E E
O Q Y F L P S G P T E D A T H
M G Z S E I R F J A C O B I I
E F A B V O D E Q S S C I M M
E D O M N E R D L I H C U S T
```

by Angela Fletcher

⚡Bonus Trivia

What group of people will be called "the children of God"?

13

C's in the Bible

CAIN
CALVARY
CANAAN
CANDACE
CENTURION
CHALDEANS
CHERETHITES
CHERUBIMS
CHOSEN
CHRISTIANS
CHRONICLES
CHURCH
CIRCUMCISED

COLOSSIANS
CONTRITE
CONVERSION
CORBAN
CORINTHIANS
COUNTENANCE
COVENANT
CREATED
CROWN
CURSE
CUSH
CYRUS

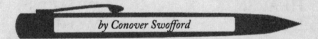

by Conover Swofford

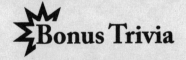

⚡Bonus Trivia

What were the Ten Commandments engraved on?

Two tables of stone. (Deuteronomy 4:13)

14

Creation

BEAST	LAND
CATTLE	LIGHT
DAY	MAN
EARTH	NIGHT
FIRMAMENT	RESTED
FISH	SEAS
FOWL	SEED
FRUIT	STARS
GOOD	TREE
GRASS	WATERS
HEAVEN	WHALES
HERB	WOMAN

```
B  R  F  E  R  S  T  R  E  S  T  E  D  H  Y
N  E  M  A  M  R  I  F  O  Z  R  Q  X  Y  G
B  E  A  S  T  M  N  N  I  T  H  G  I  L  O
G  R  A  S  S  E  E  D  N  S  W  W  S  A  O
M  W  E  H  W  A  T  E  R  S  H  A  F  N  D
T  G  F  H  N  A  M  T  R  M  E  S  T  D  N
H  E  O  H  E  A  V  E  N  S  S  H  W  O  S
G  F  E  S  M  H  A  I  H  E  M  S  O  H  M
I  L  L  R  S  R  A  T  S  T  U  A  M  R  N
N  Y  I  L  T  E  H  F  R  R  E  M  A  T  W
L  F  L  H  S  T  L  R  A  E  T  S  N  O  S
S  E  A  R  C  G  M  A  R  P  E  L  A  D  L
F  R  U  I  T  H  H  H  H  R  O  C  M  W
S  K  C  A  T  T  L  E  H  W  D  A  Y  U  O
K  S  M  L  P  Q  Z  X  X  L  M  D  F  G  F
```

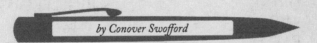

by Conover Swofford

15

The Cure for Anxiety

Matthew 6:25–34

ADD	LIFE
ARRAYED	LILIES
BARNS	LITTLE
BODY	MEAT
CAST	NEED
CLOTHED	OVEN
CUBIT	RAIMENT
DRINK	RIGHTEOUSNESS
EVIL	SEEK
FAITH	SOLOMON
FATHER	SOW
FEEDETH	SPIN
FIRST	STATURE
FOWLS	SUFFICIENT
GATHER	THOUGHT
GOD	TOIL
HEAVENLY	TOMORROW
KINGDOM	

```
R C D L D R R T Z L S G E H W
O I I E E R O L M I U H H T D
B O G H H M I O X L F T L I E
T O T H O T D N U I F E S A Y
T A D R T G O E K E I D O F A
G A R Y N E J L E S C E L O R
R O E I N R O W C N I E O W R
W K K M Q N A U F M E F M L A
T H O U G H T I S A N C O S N
L E R U T A T S M N T K N V I
I N L I T T L E T E E H E K P
F Y L N E V A E H I N S E E S
E P D V S N R A B I B T S R S
K D I U J M F I R S T U G O D
A L U J Z N E V O T S A C W W
```

by Ruth Graether

16

Old Testament Cities

AI
BABYLON
BETHEL
BETHLEHEM
DAN
GAZA
GEZER
GILGAL
GOMORRAH
HARAN
HAZOR
HEBRON
HESHBON

JERICHO
JERUSALEM
KADESH
LACHISH
PENUEL
SHECHEM
SHILOH
SIDON
SODOM
TYRE
UR
ZION

```
R  S  S  L  M  Y  X  G  E  Z  E  R  T  M  B
B  E  T  H  L  E  H  E  M  I  R  S  K  L  G
E  M  H  O  L  I  H  S  T  A  J  A  C  H  I
O  L  R  O  O  Z  K  K  A  D  E  S  H  H  L
H  E  Z  Y  A  H  A  M  A  H  R  A  E  E  G
C  G  R  O  Z  A  H  N  C  C  U  H  B  H  A
I  L  Z  Z  A  S  Y  Y  M  M  S  S  R  U  L
P  E  Z  E  G  O  M  O  R  R  A  H  O  S  B
O  U  H  Z  R  D  S  M  T  H  L  E  N  E  T
H  N  A  H  N  O  D  I  S  H  E  C  T  A  R
C  E  M  A  K  M  H  S  U  K  M  H  Y  K  L
I  P  Z  H  E  S  H  B  O  N  E  E  R  M  X
R  L  H  H  S  I  H  C  A  L  Z  M  E  P  Q
E  H  A  R  E  T  M  N  A  R  A  H  Z  Z  Y
J  G  H  E  A  Z  I  O  N  O  L  Y  B  A  B
```

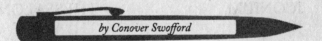

by Conover Swofford

17

New Testament Cities

AMPHIPOLIS	LAODICEA
ANTIOCH	LYSTRA
APOLLONIA	NAZARETH
ATHENS	PAPHOS
BETHSAIDA	PERGA
CAPERNAUM	PERGAMOS
CORINTH	PHILADELPHIA
DAMASCUS	PHILIPPI
EMMAUS	SARDIS
EPHESUS	SMYRNA
ICONIUM	THESSALONICA
JOPPA	THYATIRA

```
R H L M T P A D I A S H T E B
S A P O L L O N I A N R Y M S
O M H S I L O P I H P M A S O
H S N E H T A H A R A A U P M
P N J R S A R D I S C S A H A
A C O R I N T H O I E C L I G
P C P C O R S N N H A N A C R
A P P H I L Y O P A B A B A E
R P A I H P L E D A L I H P P
I S U C D A M A S C U S T E S
T R O C S I P P I L I H P R T
A M S S H L H T E R A Z A N A
Y L E L A O D I C E A A P A N
H H C O I T N A P E R G A U F
T H M U I N O C I S U A M M E
```

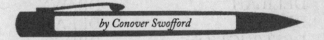

by Conover Swofford

⚡Bonus Trivia

Who held up Moses' hands at Rephidim
while Joshua battled the Amalekites?

Aaron and Hur (Exodus 17:12–13)

18

D's in the Bible

DAGON
DAMASCUS
DANCE
DANIEL
DARIUS
DARKNESS
DAUGHTERS
DAVID
DEATH
DECAPOLIS
DELILAH
DEMAS
DESTRUCTION
DEUTERONOMY
DEVIL

DINAH
DISCIPLES
DIVISIONS
DIVORCE
DOOR
DORCAS
DOUBT
DOVE
DOWRY
DRAGONS
DRAWN
DREAM
DRINK
DRUNKENNESS

```
D E S T R U C T I O N R O O D
D R D E M A S N O I S I V I D
D S U I R A D C H D N O G A D
D S D N D A N I E L D D M R M
S D A R K N E S S H Y A E V A
Z N O A M E D D A M S A D I D
H E O W S S N D O C M R D D S
A C S G R D E N U D E V I L R
L R S H A Y O S E D I N A H E
I O S Z D R A W N S S S T M T
L V S Y E R D O V E S B S D H
E I S T D A V I D D U Z Z Y G
D D U H T A E D D O R C A S U
S E L P I C S I D A N C E D A
D D E C A P O L I S K N I R D
```

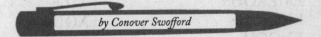
by Conover Swofford

19

E's in the Bible

EARTHQUAKE
EASTWARD
ECCLESIASTES
EDEN
EDOM
EGYPT
ELDERS
ELEVENTH
ELI
ELIAB
EMERODS
ENGINES
ENOCH
EPAPHRODITUS

EPHESIANS
EPHOD
ESAU
ESTHER
ETHIOPIA
EUNUCH
EUODIAS
EUPHRATES
EVE
EVERLASTING
EXILE
EXODUS
EYE OF A
   NEEDLE
EZRA

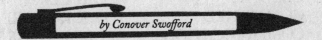
```
E  V  E  S  U  T  I  D  O  R  H  P  A  P  E
E  T  E  E  U  P  H  R  A  T  E  S  E  U  A
G  E  H  D  R  A  W  T  S  A  E  H  N  E  R
N  E  X  I  L  E  D  D  D  T  E  U  D  D  T
I  L  E  D  O  M  U  A  S  E  C  O  M  E  H
T  E  D  O  H  P  E  A  S  H  R  N  E  N  Q
S  V  S  S  N  A  I  S  E  H  P  E  M  E  U
A  E  Z  E  D  S  B  A  E  Z  L  K  E  A  A
L  N  I  S  E  A  D  S  D  E  I  R  S  K
R  T  A  L  I  H  M  H  E  D  D  Z  O  S  E
E  H  C  L  E  H  P  R  M  R  E  L  D  M  S
V  C  E  D  E  E  S  U  D  O  X  E  S  M  T
E  L  D  E  E  N  A  F  O  E  Y  E  R  M  H
D  E  N  G  I  N  E  S  E  O  T  P  Y  G  E
C  E  H  P  O  E  U  O  D  I  A  S  D  D  R
```

by Conover Swofford

20

On the Emmaus Road

Luke 24:13–32

ABIDE
ANGELS
BLESSED
BODY
BREAD
CHIEF
CHRIST
CLEOPAS
COMMUNED
COMMUNICATIONS
CONSTRAINED
EMMAUS
EYES
GOD
HEART

ISRAEL
JESUS
MOSES
PASS
PRIESTS
PROPHET
REDEEMED
RULERS
SCRIPTURES
SEPULCHRE
STRANGER
SUFFERED
VISION
WALK
WOMEN

```
S K C O N S T R A I N E D S L
H C Q D E P J R C B D K N E A
F T R S E B R O A E O O L P B
Y G O I R R M I H E I D Y U I
C M V E P M E Q E T H I Y L D
L K A I U T I F A S P S S C E
E D L N S N U C F R T U U H B
O C E A A I I R O U H S A R R
P D T V W N O P E Z S E M E E
A O L S U B H N L S Y J M D G
S G E M I E D E M E E D E R N
Y P M P T R A E S S L E G N A
W O M E N R H R U L E R S N R
C K K S S A P C F E I H C I T
P Y W I B L E S S E D V U N S
```

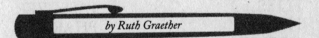

by Ruth Graether

After Saul was baptized and spent time
with other disciples, where did he go
to witness for Christ?

To the synagogues. (Acts 9:18–20)

21

Plagues of Egypt and the Passover

AARON
ASHES
BLEMISH
BLOOD
BOILS
CATTLE
DARKNESS
EGYPTIANS
FLIES
FROGS
GOSHEN
HAIL
HARDENED
HEBREWS
HORSES
HOUSEHOLD

JUDGMENT
LAMB
LICE
LOCUSTS
MAGICIANS
MEMORIAL
MOSES
ORDINANCE
PASSOVER
PHARAOH
RIVER
ROD
SACRIFICE
SERPENT
SIGNS

```
S C B S G S B S E S S W E W H
W A O N Y G P G E T G C Z M A
E T I A A D Y H S R N O E W R
R T L I D P S U S A P M R E D
B L S C T A C U N E O E V F E
E E H I T O R I C R S I N V N
H O A G L N D K I S R R N T E
P N I A I R T A N E H S O G D
S Z L M O U L N H E O K R H S
S A C R I F I C E S S F A L E
N R E V O S S A P M I S A V S
P H A R A O H F K H G M D V O
D L O H E S U O H R B D E O M
A P B L O O D S E I L F U L R
S W F S I G N S E C I L D J B
```

by Ruth Graether

⚡Bonus Trivia

Who is the only person in scripture
who is said to have sneezed?

The Shunammite woman's son. (2 Kings 4:25–35)

22

Enemies of Israel

AMALEKITES
AMORITES
ASSYRIA
BABYLONIANS
CANAANITES
CHALDEANS
CHILDREN OF
   AMMON
EDOMITES
EGYPTIANS
ETHIOPIANS
HITTITES
HIVITES
JEBUSITES

KOA
MEDES
MESOPOTAMIA
MIDIANITES
MOABITES
PEKOD
PERIZZITES
PERSIANS
PHILISTINES
ROME
SAMARITANS
SHOA
SYRIA

```
A M A A M A L E K I T E S D N M
R A M S N A I T P Y G E A O S I
S T A I M A T O P O S E M K N D
E N S H S E T I B A O M A E A I
T S A S E T I V I H A O R P I A
I E A I K M S S A F D R I F N N
Z T A H S E O O O I R E T J O I
Z I M M D R I N H T R E A E L T
I T M E Z Z E T S S S Y N B Y E
R T M T H R M P O K O A S U B S
E I T E D O M I T E S H L S A I
P H I L I S T I N E S R P I B R
Z Z I O O S N A I P O I H T E Y
C H A L D E A N S H O M E E R S
C A N A A N I T E S S S S S R S
T S S E T I R O M A I R Y S S A
```

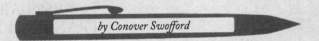

by Conover Swofford

Bonus Trivia

What unnamed woman from Samaria
did Jesus offer the "living water" to?

The woman at the well. (John 4:7, 10)

23

F's in the Bible

FAITH

FALSE

FAMINE

FASTING

FATHER

FATHERLESS

FAULTLESS

FAVOUR

FEAR OF THE
LORD

FEAST

FELIX

FELLOWSHIP

FENCED

FESTUS

FIELD

FIERY

FIFTY

FIRSTLING

FLESH

FLOOD

FLOUR

FOLLOWED

FOOTSTEPS

FORGIVEN

FOURSQUARE

FRANKINCENSE

FRINGES

FRUIT

```
S E G N I R F I R S T L I N G
S F F E I E O D E W O L L O F
S F R N Y H U Y S F A L S E M
E N E I T S R C D F F F A F F
L E D M F E S R S O R R Z E R
T V F A I L Q Z Y Y O Z L L A
L I S F F F U Y F F F L Y I N
U G S E F E A S T E O F F X K
A R S S D D R H C W L E A G I
F O O T S T E P S W N W T N N
A F R U O L F H M C W W H I C
V A F S O R I W E Z Y E E T E
O I M R U P E D S E S E R S N
U T D I M W F I E L D X X A S
R H T W S S E L R E H T A F E
```

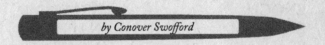

by Conover Swofford

⚡Bonus Trivia

What grew from the ground God cursed
after Adam and Eve's sin?

Thorns and thistles. (Genesis 3:17–18)

24

Fathers and Sons in Genesis

ABEL	JAPHETH
ABRAHAM	JOSEPH
ADAM	JUDAH
AMMON	LAMECH
ASHER	LEVI
BENJAMIN	LOT
CAIN	MANASSEH
DAN	METHUSELAH
ENOCH	MOAB
EPHRAIM	NAPHTALI
ESAU	NOAH
GAD	REUBEN
HAM	SETH
ISAAC	SHEM
ISHMAEL	SIMEON
JACOB	TERAH

```
T K B A O M N M J U D A H N J
E U S H E M N A I J L B H I V
I S H M A E L O D A O R T M O
I L A T H P A N M E R A E A H
H U P U K O B I T M Y H H J C
L E B A E H A O N N A A P N E
L H P E S O J T C L E M A E M
M E T H U S E L A H O B J B A
A L H E S S A N A M L T U Y L
S C P C K M I H M A H J H E W
H F D A G J C L A E R H P E R
E A D A M S A E T R C S X T X
R H A S J X I V R O E I E O C
T Z V I B E N I N S X T N T N
B O C A J N O E M I S V H W H
```

by N. Teri Grottke

25

Fathers and Sons in Exodus and Numbers

AARON	HOBAB
ABIHU	HUR
AHIEZER	IZAHAR
AHIRA	JETHRO
AHOLIAB	JOSHUA
AMMINADAB	KOHATH
AMMISHADDAI	MAHLI
AMRAM	MERARI
BEZALEEL	MOSES
ELEAZAR	MUSHI
ELIAB	NETHANEEL
ELIASAPH	NUN
ELISHAMA	OCRAN
ELIZUR	PEDAHZUR
ENAN	REUEL
GAMALIEL	SHEDEUR
GIDEONI	SHELUMIEL
HEBRON	URI
HELON	ZUAR

```
I R A R E M I K O H A T H X E
V A M U S H I G L S P M Q Q L
H U E E N A N E A E A U H E I
E Z L D C S U H D M R C I M A
B I I E U E E A R I A M L M S
R M S H R L H A A B U L M G A
O A H S O Z M C A L E I I A P
N H A N U N N D E E S D H E H
A L M R A O A H N H E O B J L
H I A R R N S A A O L A A O J
I H C A I E H D N I I R B S E
E O A M S T D I A L Z I I H T
Z B M O E A U B E K U H H U H
E A M N I Z A H A R R A U A R
R B E Z A L E E L E A Z A R O
```

by N. Teri Grottke

26

False Gods

ADRAMMELECH
ANAMMELECH
ASHTORETH
BAAL
BEELZEBUB
BRASEN SERPENT
CHEMOSH
DAGON
DIANA
EPHOD
JUPITER

LUCIFER
MERCURIUS
MILCOM
MOLECH
MOLTEN CALF
NEHUSHTAN
NERGAL
NIBHAZ
SUCCOTHBENOTH
TAMMUZ
TARTAK

```
C T N E P R E S N E S A R B P
G R M F A L T X Q Z Y F G B N
H E O N O G A D I A N A U M F
T T L C H E M O S H R B T O G
O I T S S O M H K K E S A C H
N P E H L H U P H Z U T S L C
E U N E A L Z E L H O R H I E
B J C E G E E E H G E T M L
H H A S R S E N S A H C O H E
T Z L Y E B A A L H C H R L M
O A F Y N E T A R T A K E E M
C H N E H U S H T A N H T R A
C B G X M R E F I C U L H R R
U I G M E R C U R I U S D D D
S N G R H H C E L E M M A N A
```

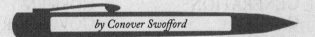

by Conover Swofford

⚡ Bonus Trivia

What did Paul tell Timothy about those who do not provide for their own households?

They have denied the faith and are worse than infidels. (1 Timothy 5:8)

27

G's in the Bible

GABRIEL
GAD
GALATIANS
GALILEE
GAMALIEL
GARMENTS
GATHER
GAZA
GEHAZI
GENEALOGIES
GENERATIONS
GENESIS
GENTILES
GENTLENESS
GETHSEMANE

GEZER
GIANTS
GIDEON
GLORY
GOD
GOG
GOLD
GOLGOTHA
GOLIATH
GOODNESS
GOSHEN
GOVERNOR
GRACE
GRAVEN IMAGE

```
G R A V E N I M A G E D L O G
R E H T A G O O D N E S S A E
G M T G E O M M R R S S H N
E R G H M S G G G T I N E T E
N H A A S H H I N S O S N O A
T Z B Z D E A E E I M E E G L
I G R Z A N M N T R A C L L O
L A I M T R E A Z Y Z A T O G
E L E S A G R Z N Z A R N G I
S I L G M E M Z G E G G E R E
G L G Z N R O N R E V O G G S
E E G E Z R H M H T A I L O G
Z E G A L A T I A N S M O D G
E G Z Z L E I L A M A G R R R
R G I D E O N H O G L R Y L G
```

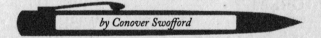

by Conover Swofford

28

Attributes of God

ALMIGHTY
BLESSED
COUNSELLOR
ENDURING
ETERNAL
EVERLASTING
FAITHFUL
GLORIFIED
GOD
GRACIOUS
GREAT
HOLY
IMMORTAL

IMMUTABLE
JUST
KIND
LIFE
LIGHT
LOVE
MERCIFUL
PEACE
RIGHTEOUS
TRUE
UPRIGHT
WISE
WONDERFUL

```
R W H Y A N U L V W G E C L R
A I L G W P U K O F N S O A T
I O G S I F E N O M I I U N R
H M C H H U D A E I R W T R O
D H M T T E C R C H U Q A E L
D E I O R E C Y T E D G E T L
E A S F R I O H T N N L R E E
F U U S F T G U K H E O G O S
J L R U E I A I S B G R R A N
T V L T L L N L T H G I R P U
E N S H Z D B T N S M F M N O
E V E R L A S T I N G I J L C
E L B A T U M M I G J E U X A
Q E V O L Y L I F E O D S Q X
G R A C I O U S O Z I D T N X
```

by Ruth Graether

⚡ Bonus Trivia

What kind of believer did Jesus liken to
a man who built his house upon a rock?

A "wise man"/one who hears and obeys Christ's sayings.
(Matthew 7:24)

29

Genealogy from Adam to Judah

ADAM
SETH
ENOS
CAINAN
MAHALALEEL
JARED
ENOCH
METHUSELAH
LAMECH
NOAH
SHEM
ARPHAXAD

SALAH
EBER
PELEG
REU
SERUG
NAHOR
TERAH
ABRAM
ISAAC
JACOB
JUDAH

```
N N A L E G E L E G G E L E P
E M N N N A N I A C G H M M E
R N H H A H G U R E S S S P L
M N O S H H H T T O P P S H G
S S S C A S R M N A H O R M E
S M H L H A R E T M Z Z I H L
J M A M M H H T S R H S E T H
A S D R A R P H A X A D A M H
R A E E B E J U D A H H A H H
E H E L L A L S C G D C U F G
D D A D C D M E H A H E J A R
E E E O O O D L H H R M E H S
O O B O N O O A H H L A S G L
R R E R M M A H A L A L E E L
S S R S S P T M M L E G L E G
```

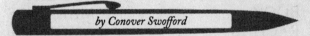

by Conover Swofford

⚡ Bonus Trivia

What man, with a name like a Roman god, became a powerful preacher of Christ in the early church?

30

Genealogy of Christ

Matthew 1:1–17

ABRAHAM	ROBOAM
ISAAC	ASA
JACOB	JOSAPHAT
JUDAS	JORAM
PHARES	OZIAS
THAMAR	JOATHAM
AMINADAB	ACHAZ
SALMON	EZEKIAS
BOOZ	MANASSES
RACHAB	AMON
OBED	JOSIAS
RUTH	ZOROBABEL
JESSE	ELEAZAR
DAVID	MATTHAN
SOLOMON	

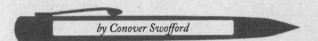

by Conover Swofford

U	Q	L	F	O	J	Z	E	E	K	M	N	P	R	T
Q	Z	S	A	I	S	O	J	R	A	Z	A	E	L	E
E	S	A	I	K	E	Z	E	U	E	O	Z	I	A	S
J	O	A	T	H	A	M	S	T	L	R	O	R	S	S
J	O	T	E	S	S	E	J	H	L	O	O	B	E	D
N	O	M	L	A	S	I	O	A	E	B	B	J	T	N
H	T	J	J	S	H	P	T	M	C	A	A	S	I	O
C	R	R	A	B	R	A	H	A	M	B	M	O	D	M
E	S	N	M	L	A	H	A	R	L	E	O	R	A	O
H	A	M	I	N	C	M	M	N	N	L	N	T	V	L
M	T	X	N	T	H	P	P	Y	X	Z	T	Z	I	O
A	S	H	A	S	A	S	E	R	A	H	P	Q	D	S
R	C	H	D	L	B	B	O	C	A	J	U	D	A	S
O	H	R	A	K	M	U	H	N	H	Z	A	H	C	A
J	R	O	B	O	A	M	J	O	S	A	P	H	A	T

31

Biblical Gifts

ALMONDS
BALM
BULLS
CAMELS
COAT
COWS
DONKEYS
EWES
FRANKINCENSE
GOATS
GOLD

HONEY
JEWELS
MYRRH
OINTMENT
RAIMENT
RAMS
SEPULCHRE
SILVER
SPICES
SPIKENARD
TREES

```
J E S U M A R J H N S R D M W
J E S M A T A O C S R S W O C
E P E X X X K H A S W O W A R
W K C D O Z L X E X A H M L A
E S I L C H I E W E S E R M I
L E P O E R R A M S L S O O M
S P S G H T E S P S K E S N E
A U M R H Y L S Y E K N O D N
H L R P E R R R B U L L S T
A Y Y N N H M L A B M M M M T
M H O A O G G O A T S T T S S
P H H E H O I N T M E N T S S
R E V L I S P I K E N A R D E
T M F R A N K I N C E N S E E
H S R R Y M E R H C L U P E S
```

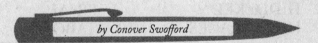

by Conover Swofford

32

Biblical Geography

ABANA
ARARAT
EBAL
EDEN
ESHCOL
EUPHRATES
GALILEE
GETHSEMANE
GIHON
HERMON
HIDDEKEL
HIGH PLACES

HOREB
JORDAN
KIDRON
MOUNT OF
   OLIVES
NEBO
PISGAH
PISON
RED SEA
RIVER OF EGYPT
SINAI
TABOR
WILDERNESS

```
S L K G M R T S S W Z L P R K
M Z S G E T H S E M A N E D E
O H A A B A N A H B F G H U N
U E S L H E K S N S R R P C O
N R H I L E K E D D I H I S S
T M E L M A E S D E R P A R I
O O L E T A R A R A P H N H P
F N L E R O B A T P H H I I S
O O M W I L D E R N E S S A N
L R B J H P S N O H I G O J J
I D R E S C H O L N A D R O J
V I S J R J O R D H H O H N O
E K B A L O L O G B J P B P R
S E C A L P H G I H L A B E S
R I V E R O F E G Y P T Z Q N
```

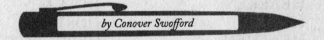

by Conover Swofford

33

H's in the Bible

HABAKKUK
HABITATION
HAGAR
HAGGAI
HAM
HANDKERCHIEFS
HARPERS
HAZOR
HEADLONG
HEALED
HEARKEN
HEART
HEATHEN
HEAVEN
HEBREWS

HELL
HEMLOCK
HENCEFORTH
HERITAGE
HIGHEST
HOLINESS
HONOUR
HOPE
HORSEMEN
HOSANNA
HOSEA
HOST
HYPOCRITES
HYSSOP

```
M H P G Z H G G N O L D A E H
H E A V E N O I T A T I B A H
O A H H H H H Y S S O P N A H
P T Z Y H E A L E D D D G M M
E H Z O A A L K U K K A B A H
S E Y R R L H M Z E R G H H H
S N K N E M E S R O H O S E A
E E Z H Y P O C R I T E S H R
N G H O M T H E A R T T M H P
I T T S S I T S S R S N N M E
L R Q H E N C E F O R T H H R
O Y Z F X S G M H E B R E W S
H O S A N N A I A G G A H X X
Y Z X T S E H G I H O N O U R
H E R I T A G E K C O L M E H
```

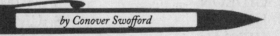

by Conover Swofford

⚡Bonus Trivia

What did Nicodemus say to Jesus'
statement that a man must have a
second birth?

34

Heroes and Heroines

ABIALBON
AHIAM
AZMAVETH
BANI
BARAK
DAVID
EHUD
ELIAHBA
ELIPHELET
GAREB
GIDEON
HEZRAI
HIDDAI
IGAL

ITTAI
JAEL
JAIR
JONATHAN
JOSHUA
JOSIAH
MOSES
NOAH
RAHAB
SAMSON
SAMUEL
SAUL
TOLA
ZELEK

```
S  A  M  S  O  N  O  E  D  I  G  G  Z  O  P
J  A  E  L  A  F  T  E  L  E  H  P  I  L  E
A  E  S  K  H  F  H  T  E  V  A  M  Z  A  G
B  E  L  E  M  O  S  E  S  D  U  H  E  Z  P
H  A  P  L  F  T  H  A  L  J  R  I  A  J  L
A  U  T  I  H  M  I  U  A  O  G  C  P  U  A
I  H  D  A  E  P  A  O  G  S  I  I  A  B  J
L  S  X  J  Z  V  T  C  I  I  D  S  I  O  G
E  O  K  D  R  S  T  E  F  A  F  A  N  K  A
R  J  A  T  A  A  I  X  V  H  L  A  E  H  T
A  G  R  A  I  M  N  I  A  B  T  L  I  O  J
H  A  A  E  X  U  D  O  O  H  E  A  L  C  Y
A  R  B  I  S  E  N  N  A  Z  M  A  W  J  M
B  E  J  U  F  L  Z  N  Q  P  N  I  N  A  B
T  B  V  F  G  M  J  W  N  H  I  D  D  A  I
```

by N. Teri Grottke

35

I's in the Bible

I AM THAT I AM
IMAGE
IMMANUEL
IMMEDIATELY
IMPOSSIBLE
IMPUTED
INCENSE
INCREASE
INDIGNATION
INGATHERING
INHERITANCE
INIQUITY
INJURED

INSPIRATION
INSTRUCTION
INSURRECTION
INTENT
INTERCESSION
INVISIBLE
INWARD
IRON
ISHMAEL
ISLAND
ISSUE
ITCH
IVORY

I	I	R	O	N	O	I	T	C	U	R	T	S	N	I
A	M	N	E	N	E	Y	T	I	U	Q	I	N	I	T
M	M	M	S	G	M	M	N	I	N	W	A	R	D	C
T	E	I	A	I	N	C	E	N	S	E	Z	X	Z	H
H	D	M	E	N	O	I	T	A	R	I	P	S	N	I
A	I	P	R	M	U	P	N	D	E	R	U	J	N	I
T	A	U	C	N	N	E	I	S	S	U	E	I	A	E
I	T	T	N	I	H	M	L	E	A	M	H	S	I	A
A	E	E	I	N	V	I	S	I	B	L	E	A	S	D
M	L	D	I	N	S	U	R	R	E	C	T	I	O	N
Y	Y	I	N	G	A	T	H	E	R	I	N	G	I	A
R	T	T	E	C	N	A	T	I	R	E	H	N	I	L
O	I	I	I	E	L	B	I	S	S	O	P	M	I	S
V	I	N	D	I	G	N	A	T	I	O	N	I	I	I
I	Q	Z	N	O	I	S	S	E	C	R	E	T	N	I

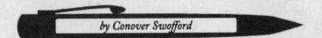

by Conover Swofford

⚡Bonus Trivia

What happened to the sky between the sixth and ninth hours as Jesus approached death?

Darkness came over the land. (Matthew 27:45–50)

36

Instruments and Songs

INSTRUMENTS:

BELLS
CORNETS
CYMBALS
DULCIMER
FLUTE
HARP
HIGH SOUNDING
INSTRUMENTS
LOUD
ORGANS
PSALTERY
SACKBUT
STRINGED
TABRETS
TIMBREL
TRUMPET

SONGS:

ANGEL
BARAK
CHENANIAH
DAVID
DEBORAH
ISAIAH
MARY
MORNING STARS
MOSES
SONG OF
SOLOMON
SONG OF THE
LORD

M O R N I N G S T A R S S C Y
C Y M T A B R E T S N A G R O
D U O L S L A B M Y C H E I D
S H H T L F Y S S H T T M N U
S A A M M R L T E I L F O S L
S R I H A L E N M A L L S T C
D O A M E N A B S T T U E R I
E B S B R N R P M U R T S U M
G E I O I E T R U M P E T M E
N D C A L D D D D I V A D E R
I K H H I G H S O U N D I N G
R K A R A B G A N G E L S T H
T H I P R A H T U B K C A S M
S O N G O F S O L O M O N H N
H S D R O L E H T F O G N O S

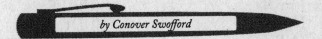

by Conover Swofford

37

J's in the Bible

JAEL
JAILOR
JAMBRES
JANNES
JAPHETH
JAPHO
JARHA
JARIB
JARMUTH
JASHER
JASON
JAVAN
JAVELIN
JEALOUS
JEDIDIAH
JEMIMA

JEOPARDY
JERUBBAAL
JERUSHAH
JESTING
JESUS
JETHRO
JEWELS
JEWRY
JOAB
JOY
JUBILE
JUDE
JUDGMENT
JUNIA
JUSTIFIED

```
O R H T E J O L B M G L E A J
J H J J J H R I A N R E D U J
E H P M J O R I I Z N H J H E
S M J A L A N T S S M T T A A
U J V I J U S T I F I E D H L
S A A J J E M I M A H J R S O
N J J J J E R U B B A A L U U
B H H H T E H P A J J R J R S
A Z Q U J U D G M J A M E E S
O J A N N E S I J H S U W J J
J A M B R E S H D K O T R O J
J R J J J A V E L I N H Y Y Y
H U Y D R A P O E J A M S M J
M T N E M G D U J A S H E R O
Z H T E L I B U J S L E W E J
```

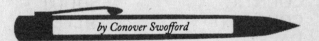

by Conover Swofford

38

The Conquest of Jericho

Joshua 6:1

ARK
BRASS
CITY
COMPASS
CONSECRATED
COUNTRY
COVENANT
DAY
FOUNDATION
GATES
GOLD
ISRAEL
JOSHUA
KINDRED
LIVE
LORD

MESSENGERS
PEOPLE
PRIESTS
RAHAB
SEVEN
SHOUT
SILVER
SPIES
TREASURY
TRUMPETS
VALOUR
VESSELS
VOICE
WAR
WORD

```
M C U Y I E I P S W D R V N G
Q O A T A S D S O E X D A G R
M V K U A D R R T S Q L L A S
N E F O U N D A T I O N O T U
R N S H V E R S E V O S U E O
A A Y S V C E N E L H F R S W
W N M I E I O S C O U N T R Y
Y T L S R N S L R S P I E S K
Q R N P S E G N G O L D A S I
Q O U G L S T E P M U R T S N
C J O S H U A K R A N E V A D
I K M C A Q L R B S E V P P R
T E L P O E P O B D V L Q M E
Y E C I O V R Q R X E I O O D
B A H A R X T T L D S S R C U
```

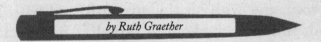

by Ruth Graether

⚡ Bonus Trivia

How did Ahab greet the prophet Elijah when he called on the king during an extended drought?

"Art thou he that troubleth Israel?" (1 Kings 18:16–17)

39

A Lawyer Tempts Jesus

Luke 10:25–29

And, **behold**, a **certain lawyer stood** up, and **tempted** him, saying, **Master**, what shall I do to **inherit** eternal life? He **said** unto **him**, What is **written** in the **law**? how **readest** thou? And he **answering** said, Thou shalt **love** the **Lord** thy **God** with all thy **heart**, and with all thy **soul**, and with all thy **strength**, and with all thy **mind**; and thy neighbour as **thyself**. And he said unto him, **Thou** hast answered **right**: this do, and thou shalt **live**. But he, **willing** to **justify himself**, said unto Jesus, And who is my neighbour?

```
Y F I T S U J R G I S D T L L
A W Z T N R O I N L H E H O U
L J R M R B C H I Y I T G V O
C T I I H A E J R P M P I E S
L N S G T R E U E A S M R B E
D O I E I T O H W N E E H F V
M E R T D H E P S I L T L I M
N O L D T A C N N R F E D X M
D I A S E K E E A Q S O L B S
G O D W D F R R R Y O A A E A
T S T R E N G T H T W H W H A
L I P K U X A T S Y A T X O O
L P P X D P N P E F J I N L F
W I L L I N G R U H T P N D Q
L I V E B X B W R E T S A M Z
```

by Ruth Graether

Why was the woman at the well surprised
when Jesus spoke to her?

He was a Jew; she was a Samaritan. (John 4:9)

40

Judges and
Their Helpers

ABDON
ANGEL
BARAK
CHILDREN [OF]
  ISRAEL
DAGGER
DEBORAH
EHUD
ELON
FLEECE
FOXES
GIDEON
IBZAN
JAEL
JAIR
JAWBONE

JEPHTHAH
JERUBBAAL
LAD
LAMPS
MESSENGERS
OTHNIEL
OX GOAD
PITCHERS
SAMSON
SHAMGAR
SPIRIT [OF THE]
  LORD
TEN THOUSAND
THREE
  HUNDRED
TOLA
TRUMPETS

```
T M N O S M A S R A G M A H S
S R E G N E S S E M P S T S S
T M I S R A E L T S A P G P T
E P B E P K C T S N T I I M M
P I Z X T A E S G M T R D A P
M T A O M R E E T P E I E L D
U C N F P A L E I N H T O L A
R H T S C B F A Z O U R N J O
T E N T H O U S A N D O X A G
Z R Z R I A J B A B A K Q W X
T S M X L X H A R O B E D B O
P S D T D A G G E R L U U O L
M A P M R X A B D O N U R N E
L T H R E E H U N D R E D E A
T M P S N Z X H A H T H P E J
```

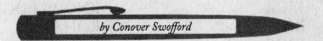

by Conover Swofford

41

K's in the Bible

KABZEEL
KEEP
KENITE
KERCHIEFS
KERENHAPPUCH
KERNELS
KETTLE
KETURAH
KEYS
KEZIA
KICK
KIDNEYS
KIDS
KILL
KINDLED

KINDNESS
KINDRED
KINE
KINGDOM
KINSWOMAN
KISH
KISS
KNEES
KNOCK
KNOW
KNOWLEDGE
KOHATH
KORAH
KOZ

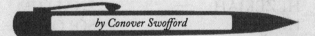

by Conover Swofford

⚡ Bonus Trivia

How much money was Judas promised for betraying Jesus?

Thirty pieces of silver. (Matthew 26:14–15)

42

Kings and Queens of Israel and Judah

AHAB
AHAZIAH
AMAZIAH
AMON
ASA
ATHALIAH
BAASHA
DAVID
HEZEKIAH
HOSHEA
JEHOAHAZ
JEHOSHAPHAT
JEHU
JEROBOAM

JEZEBEL
JOASH
JOSIAH
MANASSEH
OMRI
PEKAHIAH
REHOBOAM
SAUL
SHALLUM
SOLOMON
TIBNI
ZACHARIAH
ZEDEKIAH
ZIMRI

```
H A H A I L A H T A R O M R I
R M A N A S S E H A I Z A H A
E L E B E Z E J S H A L L U M
H I R O M I H H A I H A K E P
O L N Z Q M S O L O M O N H A
B S T B A R O A H J H H D A H
O A Z R I I H E Z E K I A H H
A M A S Z T X A H H H H V H H
M A H S A R A I I U R S I T A
A O A S H U S R R R R R D H I
E B O M M A L H A S A A A H K
H O H T A H P A H S O H E J E
S R E R A M A Z I A H E C H D
O E J S S S O H H B A H A A E
H J O A S H H N H A I S O J Z
```

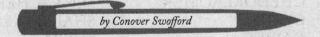

by Conover Swofford

Bonus Trivia

How did young Samson demonstrate his strength while going through the vineyard at Timnath?

By killing a lion. (Judges 14:5–6)

43

Pagan Kings and Queens

ADONIZEDEC
AHASUERUS
ARIOCH
ARTAXERXES
BALAK
BELSHAZZAR
BERA
BIRSHA
CHEDORLAOMER
CYRUS
DARIUS
DEBIR
EGLON
HEROD

HOHAM
JABIN
JAPHIA
MELCHIZEDEK
NEBUCHADNEZZAR
NECHO
PHARAOH
PIRAM
SENNACHERIB
SHALMANESER
SHEBA
SHEMEBER
SHINAB
TIDAL

```
H E R O D R A Z Z A H S L E B
R A Z Z E N D A H C U B E N C
E E M S S E X R E X A T R A E
M M S R E B E M E H S R O D D
O O K E I N G P A S S Q U E E
A H R B N N H S D E B I R E Z
L C S A N A U H N L A D I T I
R E A O R E M N S H I N A B N
O N L A R B A L A K R A N N O
D G O U O C H A A I H P A J D
E H S H H J O B O H C O I R A
H A B E H S H A P Q S Y Z Y R
C A R E B I R S H A X X R X I
R I M E L C H I Z E D E K U U
B E L S M A R I P N I B A J S
```

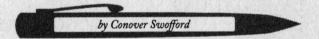

by Conover Swofford

⚡Bonus Trivia

Why did Philip leave his great work in Samaria to travel the road from Jerusalem to Gaza?

He was directed by an angel to do so. (Acts 8:25–26)

44

L's in the Bible

LABAN	LAW
LABOURERS	LAYING ON OF
LACE	HANDS
LACK	LEAH
LADDER	LEAVENED
LAKE	LEFTHANDED
LAKUM	LEPROSY
LAMB	LEVIATHAN
LAME	LIAR
LAMECH	LIFE
LAMENTATIONS	LIGHT
LAMP	LONGSUFFERING
LANCET	LOT
LAND	LOVE
LANGUAGE	LUCIFER
LASCIVIOUSNESS	LUCRE

```
L A Y I N G O N O F H A N D S
Y U T H G I L A M E C H T S D
L S C L E M A L A K E E E R E
L N O I M Z D X X L C N L E D
O O S R F S D T S N S A U R N
T I M H P E E P A U M H C U A
L T L D C E R L O P O T R O H
L A B A N L L I L L O A E B T
I T L L A V L T S S I L A F
A N M H T I P I L N E V O L E
R E O O C L L L E A H E F I L
S M L S D E N E V A E L A M B
M A A N L M L A W L L K C A L
A L A N G U A G E L A K U M L
H L G N I R E F F U S G N O L
```

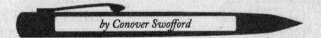

by Conover Swofford

45

The Raising of Lazarus

John 11:1–38

ABODE
ASK
AWAKE
BETHANY
BROTHER
CHRIST
DEATH
DISCIPLES
GLORIFIED
GLORY
GOD
GRAVE
HOURS
JERUSALEM
JESUS
JUDEA

LAZARUS
LIGHT
LIVETH
LORD
LOVEST
MAN
MARTHA
MARY
OINTMENT
RESURRECTION
SICK
STONE
THOMAS
TWELVE
WALK
WEEPING

```
H B N V G J L B I B E S E S B
T T N O U L R I M E N E V I J
E B H D I O O E G T A L A D Z
V K E O T T L R H H M P R B W
I A A H M A C L Y A T I G O D
L Y E W S A O E E N F C M C E
A R C U A R S I R Y C S O H D
V D R T D G Y Z N R W I K R O
D E A T H O N N H T U D E I B
J G L O R I F I E D M S J S A
S U R A Z A L B P V K E E T H
W Z J M A R T H A E L C N R O
A T S E V O L D W K E E I T U
L E N O T S J E S U S W W S R
K M M H H X E A Y R A M N T S
```

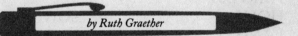

by Ruth Graether

⚡Bonus Trivia

What words did Jesus use when He
committed His mother to John's care?

"Behold thy mother!" (John 19:25–27)

46

Land Sabbaths

Leviticus 25

ACCORD

FIELD

FORTY

FRUIT

GATHER

GRAPES

GROWETH

HARVEST

HOLY

LAND

LORD

MEAT

NINE

NOT

OWN

PRUNE

REAP

REST

SABBATH

SEVEN

SEVENTH

SIX

SOW

UNDRESSED

VINE

VINEYARD

YEAR

YEARS

```
N G C H R E S T L D M T W T H
I R I S R A E Y R U P O Y V T
M A H T O R G A N R S L X W N
N P M E B V Y F U V O H L G E
O E Q N I E N N F H A Q W A V
T S X N N E O D R X R Q S E E
V E E I V X R I V L E T Q T S
O B V E N T I E M H E V Y I D
S W S B Y D S C T E P I P U R
V I N D W T L A T X A A F R O
U L R W C G G N I N E T C F C
Y O A P H T E W O R G Q C Q C
L E B N D E S S E R D N U R A
Q Y A F D Y K L H T A B B A S
N X W R O X I S O E O F O I D
```

by N. Teri Grottke

Bonus Trivia

Who were the three sons of Noah?

47

Rivers, Seas, Lakes, and Brooks

ABANA
AHAVA
ARNON
BESOR
CEDRON
CHEBAR
CHERITH
DEFENCE
EGYPT
ESHCOL
ETHIOPIA
EUPHRATES
FIRE
GAASH
GAD
GALILEE
GENNESARET

GIHON
GOZAN
GREAT
HIDDEKEL
JABBOK
KANAH
KIDRON
KISHON
KISON
LIFE
PISON
RED
SALT
TIBERIAS
ULAI
ZERED

```
C K H G X D E F E N C E J G N
L I F E I U T C N H L A H A V
E S R R G L E L T P B W Z L P
U O E A A D E I A B F O L I L
P N D G R B R A O S G I S L W
H P T O N E E K D P B A R E T
R E N I H O J H I L G H E E E
A H G C B O R S C I P A R S R
T I I A R E O D H A K V E H A
E N P D A N R O I K R A A C S
S A O O D S N I X K A N T O E
G N U H I E H S A V B N O L N
O A E U S H K R O S E B A N N
M B I B F I T E T P Y G E H E
R A I A L U K E L Z E R E D G
```

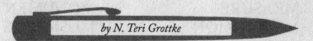

by N. Teri Grottke

48

M's in the Bible

MAGICIANS
MAGISTRATE
MAGNIFICENCE
MAGNIFY
MAGOG
MAJESTY
MANNA
MARANATHA
MEADOW
MEAL
MEASURE
MEDITATION
MEEKNESS

MENE
MERCHANDISE
MERCIES
METHUSALEH
MICHAEL
MIDDLEMOST
MIRIAM
MIZPAH
MONEY
MONEYCHANGERS
MONUMENTS
MUSICIANS
MYSTERIES

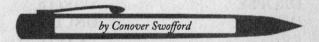

by Conover Swofford

Bonus Trivia

Whom did Elijah revive from the dead at the home of the widow in Zarephath?

Her son. (1 Kings 17:9, 20–22)

49

Miracles of Healing

BLOOD
BLIND
BOWED
BROKENHEARTED
BRUISED
DEAF
DEATH
DELIVERANCE
DEVILS
DISEASE
DROPSY
DUMB
EVIL
FEVER
HALT

IMPOTENT
INFIRMITY
ISSUE
LAME
LEPROSY
MAIMED
PALSY
PLAGUE
SICK
SIN
SPIRITS
UNCLEAN
VEXED
WITHERED

```
E G I S S U E E Y H T A E D S
I T N D I L P S S M S B A I A
A B U I E F P D S A R U K Q W
K M R O D O W U Y U E E M A L
B I N O R O N I I F I S A Q E
Y A S D K C O S T M E F I C M
H T D S L E E L P H Y V N D A
S U I E N D N O B S E A E F I
X T A M T U T H O X R R D R M
E N I Z R E E R E E Y E E K E
T V W R N I P D V A V S C D D
S L I T I E F I E I R I L F P
I W A L L P L N L W S T S A Z
N F H H O E S S I Z O N E E P
B L I N D P L A G U E B M D C
```

by N. Teri Grottke

50

Miracles Received (by)

ANDREW
ARIEL
BARTHOLOMEW
BARTIMAEUS
BETHSAIDA
CANA
CENTURION
CHILDREN
CHORAZIN
JAIRUS
JAMES
JOANNA
JOHN
JUDAS
JUDEA

LAZARUS
LEBBAEUS
LEGION
MAGDALA
MALCHUS
MARY
MULTITUDE
NAIN
PAUL
PETER
PHILIP
SAMARITAN
SERVANT
SIMON

```
K N E B Y Z N H C I C I M M X
N Z O R A O A H L A Z A R U S
N A A I I R I D N M L I E L I
I M T G R L T A I C V L T T N
Z J E I D U S I H A U E E I H
A L O R R U T U M A S A P T O
R O E A Z A S N P A N H S U J
O N M A N S M A E D E U T D C
H S N A E N R A R C E U X E Q
C N I M G I A E S A R Y S J B
A N A M E D W M B P H I L I P
Z J S L O Y A B L J U D E A D
S A D U J N E L T N A V R E S
C F I L M L X J A I R U S C A
B F B A R T H O L O M E W Q R
```

by N. Teri Grottke

⚡Bonus Trivia

What miracle occurred in the heavens the day Joshua and the Israelites defeated the armies of the five kings of the Amorites?

51

Famous Biblical Mates

ABRAM, SARAI, [AND] HAGAR
ADAM [AND] EVE
AHASUERUS [AND] ESTHER
AMRAM [AND] JOCHEBED
ANANIAS [AND] SAPPHIRA
AQUILA [AND] PRISCILLA
BOAZ [AND] RUTH
DAVID [AND] BATHSHEBA
ISAAC [AND] REBEKAH
JACOB, RACHEL, [AND] LEAH
JUDAH [AND] TAMAR
MOSES [AND] ZIPPORAH
SAMSON [AND] DELILAH
ZACHARIAS [AND] ELISABETH

A D E L I L A H A R O P P I Z
H D Z H P Z Z H H S M J D A P
A N A J H J J M E H U D C D H
S O M M A N N S M D I H H D J
U S C Z K Z O P A V A Z E V E
E M A X E M Y H A R A C H E L
R A A Z B Z Z D I O X X A H I
U S S L E A H A B R A M G H S
S M I A R A S H O R A M A T A
P A H C H C H C C H T U R H B
P R I S C I L L A Q U I L A E
P M E S T H E R J Q U I X Z T
P A D E B E H C O J I A H M H
P L L L M N A B E H S H T A B
P S A I N A N A R I H P P A S

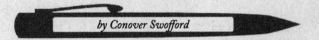

by Conover Swofford

⚡Bonus Trivia

James indicated we do not receive from
God at times for what reason?

52

Biblical Mothers and Sons

ABEL	JEZEBEL
AHAZIAH	JOCHEBED
ASENATH	JOHN
ASHER	LEAH
BATHSHEBA	MARY
BENJAMIN	MOSES
BILHAH	OBED
BOAZ	RACHEL
DAN	RAHAB
ELISABETH	RUTH
EPHRAIM	SAMUEL
EUNICE	SARAH
EVE	SIMEON
GERSHOM	SOLOMON
HANNAH	TIMOTHY
ISAAC	ZILPAH
JAMES	ZIPPORAH

```
O M V Z S Q S H A M H Q S Z Y
L M I E M O T B B O T E I I R
N E M A L U E I Z H E C M K A
L A U O R H L A K S B I E Z M
J E M M S H O M P R A N O I J
R O A H A B P F Q E S U N P E
N O T H B S Q E A G I E O P Z
B A H A Z I A H A S L B Z O E
B E T I M O T H Y D E V C R B
H A N N A H M O S E S N A A E
R R O J J O C H E B E D A H L
L E A H A P L I Z O C B S T G
L E H H D M H A R A S Y I B H
Z N B S A A I K L E H C A R B
E V E A A B N N A J J O H N C
```

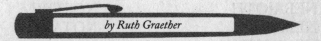

by Ruth Graether

53

N's in the Bible

NABAL	NEST
NAHOR	NETHINIM
NAHUM	NETTLES
NAME	NEVERTHELESS
NAPKIN	NICOLAITANES
NATIONS	NIMROD
NATIVITY	NINEVEH
NAUGHTY	NOAH
NAVEL	NOBLEMAN
NAZARITE	NOISOME
NEBAJOTH	NOSTRILS
NEBAT	NOTABLE
NECESSITY	NOTWITHSTANDING
NEIGHBOUR	NOURISHMENT

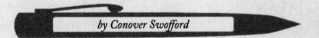

```
N  N  N  S  E  N  A  T  I  A  L  O  C  I  N
E  Y  Y  T  I  V  I  T  A  N  I  K  P  A  N
V  E  T  I  R  A  Z  A  N  A  M  E  B  N  O
E  Z  N  H  X  A  B  R  D  N  N  A  O  A  U
R  H  E  M  G  R  N  O  A  H  L  I  N  M  R
T  X  T  U  N  U  R  H  N  E  S  T  N  E  I
H  X  T  H  Z  M  A  A  T  O  N  E  N  L  S
E  S  L  A  I  R  R  N  M  E  T  Z  E  B  H
L  L  E  N  S  J  S  E  B  H  X  V  N  O  M
E  I  S  N  O  S  L  A  I  T  A  B  E  N  E
S  R  Z  X  X  B  J  N  S  N  O  I  T  A  N
S  T  M  J  A  O  I  N  I  N  E  V  E  H  T
R  S  M  T  T  M  Y  T  I  S  S  E  C  E  N
Q  O  O  H  H  R  N  E  I  G  H  B  O  U  R
G  N  I  D  N  A  T  S  H  T  I  W  T  O  N
```

by Conover Swofford

⚡Bonus Trivia

What captain in Deborah's army is listed
in Hebrews as a hero of faith, among those
who "quenched the violence of fire"?

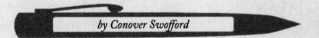

Barak. (Judges 4:14–15; Hebrews 11:32–34)

54

Noah's Descendants

ARAM

ARPHAXAD

ASSHUR

CANAAN

CUSH

ELAM

GOMER

HAM

HUL

JAPHETH

JAVAN

JOKTAN

LUD

MADAI

MAGOG

MESHECH

MIZRAIM

OBAL

OPHIR

PELEG

PHUT

SALAH

SHEM

TIRAS

TUBAL

UZ

S	M	N	E	H	U	L	M	N	M	A	D	A	I	Y
A	H	O	D	F	R	Q	J	O	K	T	A	N	X	Z
A	L	E	C	E	T	V	L	E	L	A	M	H	R	A
R	E	P	M	G	S	E	S	O	A	B	I	I	L	J
P	J	O	B	O	N	X	J	C	Z	U	Z	J	U	A
H	G	Q	B	H	A	Y	T	U	Y	C	R	K	T	V
A	I	A	A	I	A	P	H	S	X	D	A	O	I	A
X	L	R	Z	J	N	E	G	H	W	H	I	P	R	N
A	H	T	U	B	A	L	F	P	V	T	M	H	H	D
D	U	S	Y	K	C	E	E	Q	U	E	I	I	A	C
P	G	L	U	D	R	G	A	S	S	H	U	R	L	H
A	R	T	P	L	Q	Z	D	M	T	P	G	L	A	E
C	M	E	S	H	E	C	H	A	S	A	F	Y	S	S
D	E	U	W	M	U	A	C	R	R	J	E	N	Q	F
H	A	M	V	N	O	T	M	A	G	O	G	O	P	G

by Angela Fletcher

⚡Bonus Trivia

What two foods were said to flow in the land of Canaan?

Milk and honey. (Numbers 13:17, 27)

55

The Great Flood

Genesis 7:1–24

AIR

ARK

BREATH

CLEAN BEAST

COMMANDED

CREEPETH

EARTH

FEMALE

FLOOD

FORTY DAYS

FORTY NIGHTS

FOWLS

HAM

JAPHETH

LIFE

LORD

MALE

MAN

NOAH

NOT CLEAN

RAIN

RIGHTEOUS

SEED

SEVENS

SHEM

SONS

TWO AND TWO

WATERS

WINDOWS

```
F O R T Y N I G H T S A B C A
D L O R D M A L E S E V E N S
F O R T Y D A Y S J K L C M A
N F L O O D W A T E R S L P I
F N O T C L E A N U S H E M R
E T V W X Y B R E A T H A Z C
M A R A I N B C S E V E N H O
A E D E A F S U L G H I B T M
L F J M K W O S W L M A E E M
E I O P O E N P O Q R S A H A
T L U D T V S E F K X Y S P N
Z A N H B C D E E H A M T A D
F I G G H E A R T H I K L J E
W I D E E S C R E E P E T H D
R N T W O A N D T W O N O A H
```

by Angela Fletcher

What constrained Paul to appeal to the Romans to present themselves as a "living sacrifice. . .unto God"?

The mercies of God. (Romans 12:1)

56

O's in the Bible

OAK
OATH
OBEDIENCE
OBLATIONS
OBSCURE
OBSERVATION
OCCASIONS
OCCUPATION
ODIOUS
ODOUR
OFFEND
OFFICE
OFFSCOURING
OFFSPRING

OLYMPAS
OMAR
OMEGA
OMNIPOTENT
ONAN
ONESIPHORUS
ONIONS
OPENED
OPERATION
OPHIR
OPINION
OPPORTUNITY
OPPOSITIONS
OPPRESS

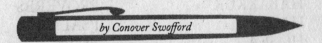

```
O B S C U R E M N O I N I P O
A R A G E M O C C A S I O N S
T N Y N N U O M A R O P P R U
H A O I A Q M M U D N E F F O
S N L R N E C N E I D E B O I
U O Y P O R H C O R U O D O D
R I M S Y T I N U T R O P P O
O T P F O F O O D E N E P O B
H A A F F N O I T A R E P O L
P P S O F F S C O U R I N G A
I U M H H O P P R E S S S S T
S C O N I O N S R I H P O T I
E C H S S T N E T O P I N M O
N O I T A V R E S B O O A K N
O P P O S I T I O N S X O D S
```

by Conover Swofford

⚡ Bonus Trivia

Whose tomb was marked by a pillar
erected by her husband, Jacob?

Rachel's. (Genesis 35:19–20)

57

Old Testament Books

AMOS
CHRONICLES
DANIEL
DEUTERONOMY
ECCLESIASTES
ESTHER
EXODUS
EZEKIEL
EZRA
GENESIS
HABAKKUK
HAGGAI
HOSEA
ISAIAH
JEREMIAH
JOB
JOEL
JONAH
JOSHUA

JUDGES
KINGS
LAMENTATIONS
LEVITICUS
MALACHI
MICAH
NAHUM
NEHEMIAH
NUMBERS
OBADIAH
PROVERBS
PSALMS
RUTH
SAMUEL
SONG OF
    SOLOMON
ZECHARIAH
ZEPHANIAH

```
J  O  E  L  M  M  B  I  H  C  A  L  A  M  E  J
H  H  L  A  M  E  N  T  A  T  I  O  N  S  X  O
A  B  O  J  E  R  E  M  I  A  H  R  O  S  O  S
I  S  E  L  C  I  N  O  R  H  C  M  P  I  D  H
A  L  R  E  H  T  S  E  P  S  A  L  M  S  U  J
S  Y  S  E  T  S  A  I  S  E  L  C  C  E  S  O
I  M  G  R  U  T  H  A  I  M  E  H  E  N  Z  N
S  O  N  G  O  F  S  O  L  O  M  O  N  E  E  A
B  N  O  I  A  G  G  A  H  H  O  J  A  G  P  H
R  R  A  K  I  N  G  S  M  I  C  A  H  X  H  L
E  E  U  H  A  B  A  K  K  U  K  M  U  O  A  E
V  T  H  J  U  D  G  E  S  R  E  B  M  U  N  I
O  U  S  S  U  C  I  T  I  V  E  L  G  E  I  N
R  E  O  G  E  N  I  H  A  I  D  A  B  O  A  A
P  D  J  M  A  R  Z  E  C  H  A  R  I  A  H  D
H  O  S  E  A  X  J  O  T  L  E  I  K  E  Z  E
```

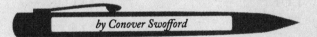

by Conover Swofford

58

New Testament Books

ACTS
COLOSSIANS
CORINTHIANS
EPHESIANS
FIRST
GALATIANS
HEBREWS
JAMES
JOHN
JUDE
LUKE
MARK

MATTHEW
PETER
PHILEMON
PHILIPPIANS
REVELATION
ROMANS
SECOND
THESSALONIANS
THIRD
TIMOTHY
TITUS

```
T H I A N S S T H I R D T T Y
H S N A I H T N I R O C M G R
S N F Y H T O M I T R E S A A
N A E P H E S I A N S I E L C
A I G S L H B R A M H S C A H
I S P S M T S R I F T N O T N
N S E E L L O O E T T A N I O
O O T M K R A M E W S I D A I
L L J A S H W A B O S P S N T
A O N J A N E N C Z O P R S A
S C U P S H H S E H H I E M L
S D P U T O T X E K U L T U E
E P T O J E T X R M G I E K V
H I M R W N A A C T S H P M E
T O T S N O M E L I H P S L R
```

by Conover Swofford

59

Biblical Occupations and Titles

ARMOURBEARER
BAKER
COMMANDER
DAUGHTER
FATHER
FISHER
HARLOT
HUNTER
HUSBANDRY
JAILOR
JUDGE
KING
LAWYER
MASON

MESSENGER
MINISTER
PRIEST
PRINCE
PROPHET
PUBLICAN
SAILOR
SCRIBE
SHEPHERD
SINGER
SON
STEWARD
WIFE

```
B X M P D R S R Z S S J E C P
M Q N I E R E I H L F A R O U
T O P H N T A E N I Z I E M B
S S T Z H I P W S G M L G M L
G A E G P H S H E A E O N A I
F N U I E K E T S T R R E N C
K A I R R R W O E V S W S D A
D R D K B P N Z M R W E S E N
F Y H A R L O T Y F B B E R R
H J M Y R D N A B S U H M R O
I U E C N I R P O L U M E E L
L D N T E H P O R P V O F K I
O G Q T R R E Y W A L N I A A
T E C R E S C R I B E E W B S
A R M O U R B E A R E R B A R
```

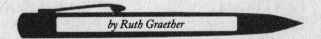

by Ruth Graether

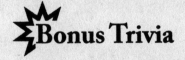

⚡Bonus Trivia

How did the Jewish leaders know where to
find Jesus in the Garden of Gethsemane?

Judas led them to Jesus. (John 18:2–3, 5)

60

P's in the Bible

PALACE
PAMPHYLIA
PARABLE
PARADISE
PARTICULAR
PARTITION
PATRIARCHS
PATRIMONY
PEARLS
PELETHITES
PENTECOST
PEOPLE
PERES

PESTILENCE
PHARISEES
PLAGUES
PLOWSHARES
PONTIUS PILATE
POTTER
PRAYER
PREACHED
PRIESTS
PRISCILLA
PROPHESYING
PUBLICANS

```
P  G  N  I  Y  S  E  H  P  O  R  P  P  S  P
P  E  N  T  E  C  O  S  T  T  E  A  E  E  A
R  L  S  T  S  E  I  R  P  O  T  R  S  T  M
S  B  A  E  C  A  L  A  P  R  A  T  T  I  P
S  A  L  S  S  R  S  L  I  H  L  I  I  H  H
P  R  L  P  P  R  E  M  S  P  I  C  L  T  Y
P  A  I  X  Z  X  O  W  U  E  P  U  E  E  L
H  P  C  P  P  N  O  B  P  A  S  L  N  L  I
A  A  S  H  Y  L  L  R  S  R  U  A  C  E  A
R  R  I  P  P  I  M  M  L  I  R  E  P  X
I  A  R  L  C  T  S  S  P  S  T  X  Y  R  Z
S  D  P  A  R  T  I  T  I  O  N  Z  X  A  T
E  I  N  N  N  R  E  T  T  O  P  T  Y  T
E  S  H  C  R  A  I  R  T  A  P  E  R  E  S
S  E  U  G  A  L  P  D  E  H  C  A  E  R  P
```

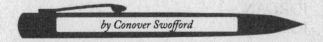

by Conover Swofford

Bonus Trivia

Where did Abraham almost sacrifice his
son Isaac?

Jehovahjireh. (Genesis 22:9–14)

61

The Promised Land

ABRAHAM
ACHAN
ALTAR
ARK
CANAAN
GIANTS
GIBEON
GRAPES
HONEY
ISRAEL
JORDAN
JOSHUA

MIGHTY MEN
MILK
MOSES
POMEGRANATES
PRIEST
RAHAB
SPY
STONES
TRIBES
VALOR
WAR

```
G T J U L O P A Q X Z Y T T R
G J O Q C A N A A N P H R S N
I P P X Z B H T S T O N E S S
B R R S P R I E S T M S R R R
E C L B J A W C S R E H R A R
O Y E N O H A R T I G L T V L
N B Y B R A R K N B R L X A S
I A Y Y D M E E A E A Y Y L T
T U R P A E M R D S N H A O N
E H T T N Y P N N A M A R A
S S R S T R S R E S T R S R I
K O G H G R R S C S E P A R G
L J G A C H A N S Z S E Y P S
I I S R A E L X E Z E C C R G
M O S E S T T X D A H A R R G
```

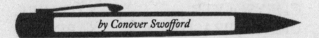

by Conover Swofford

⚡Bonus Trivia

Where did Peter go to join other believers when he was delivered from Herod's prison?

The house of Mary, mother of John Mark. (Acts 12:7–12)

62

Precious Stones, Metals, and Jewelry

AGATE
AMETHYST
BDELLIUM
BERYL
BRACELET
BRASS
CHAIN
CHALCEDONY
CHRYSOLYTE
CHRYSOPRASUS
COLLAR
DIAMOND
EARRING
EMERALD

FRONTLET
GOLD
JACINTH
JASPER
LIGURE
ONYX
ORNAMENTS
RING
SAPPHIRE
SARDIUS
SARDONYX
SILVER
TOPAZ

```
Z X K S U S A R P O S Y R H C
O N Y X E L G M U I L L E D B
Z K J E T E N F G R E P S A J
S Q Z A Y D I A M O N D F H K
S L T R L L R E E T E S T T A
A X E R O A Z Y X Y A T P N M
R Y L I S R P P N G G N C I E
B N E N Y E Z O N O A E O C T
O O C G R M D A N L T M L A H
L D A C H E B R P D E A L J Y
Y R R C C H R Y A O P N A U S
R A B L I G U R E T T R R H T
E S A P P H I R E H H O X J L
B H S A R D I U S S I L V E R
C H A I N T E L T N O R F A B
```

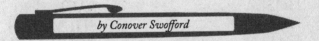

by Conover Swofford

With what words did Isaiah accept God's
call to service the year King Uzziah died?

"Here am I; send me." (Isaiah 6:1, 8)

63

Prophets

AARON
AHIJAH
AMITTAI
ANNA
DAUGHTERS
ELIJAH
ELISHA
GAD
HABAKKUK
HAGGAI
HOSEA
IDDO
ISAIAH
JEHU
JEREMIAH
JESUS
JOHN
MAN WALKING
MESSENGERS
MICAH
MICAIAH
MOSES
NATHAN
ODED
SAMUEL
SAUL
SHEMAIAH
YOUNG MAN
ZECHARIAH

S	E	L	I	S	H	A	J	I	H	A	M	A	H	H
M	H	E	L	H	E	A	I	S	A	I	A	H	M	Q
T	D	D	D	O	D	D	I	D	D	D	A	G	L	Z
M	I	S	H	N	O	R	A	A	R	I	X	X	E	Z
D	H	H	H	I	A	T	T	I	M	A	Z	Z	U	E
Y	A	I	M	T	N	D	D	E	O	E	E	E	M	C
O	D	E	D	M	H	A	R	H	S	R	H	A	A	H
U	A	X	N	Y	O	E	D	H	E	S	N	S	S	A
N	U	Z	A	H	J	E	S	U	S	W	L	A	H	R
G	G	L	H	A	A	E	L	H	A	L	L	U	A	I
M	H	H	T	J	N	M	H	L	L	L	L	L	I	A
A	T	E	A	I	T	N	K	U	K	K	A	B	A	H
N	E	H	N	L	T	I	A	G	G	A	H	H	C	H
M	R	L	T	E	N	A	E	S	O	H	A	C	I	M
T	S	R	E	G	N	E	S	S	E	M	T	T	M	M

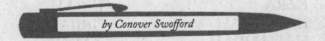

by Conover Swofford

⚡Bonus Trivia

What title was used by the voice from heaven to describe Jesus following His baptism?

"My beloved Son." (Matthew 3:16–17)

64

Priests

ABIATHAR
AHIMELECH
AMARIAH
AZARIAH
BILGAI
ELEAZAR
ELI
ELIAKIM
ELIASHIB
ELISHAMA
EZRA
HANANIAH
HASHABIAH
HILKIAH

JEHOIADA
JETHRO
MAASEIAH
MAAZIAH
MATTAN
MICHAIAH
MINIAMIN
POTIPHERAH
SERAIAH
SHEREBIAH
URIAH
URIJAH
ZADOK

```
H A D A I O H E J H A I R U H
U R I J A H A R E H P I T O P
E E E B A A A L T S S I M J H
E L L I I I E H H H E A N J A
E I L L I A E Z R A R B S H S
L A E G Z Z A D O K A I H A H
L S H A I K L I H H I A E I A
H H R I M A T T A N A T R N B
A I A M A A S E I A H H E A I
I B Z U A U H Z Z J H A B N A
A U A U Z H A S A M A R I A H
H S R S I S S T I R M M A H M
C M I K A I L E L L H H H A I
I H A C H H H C E L E M I H A
M C H C H C H N I M A I N I M
```

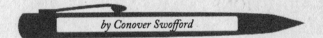

by Conover Swofford

by Conover Swofford

⚡Bonus Trivia

What was Moses doing when God spoke
to him in the flaming bush?

Herding his father-in-law's sheep. (Exodus 3:1–4)

65

Q's in the Bible

QUAILS
QUAKE
QUAKING
QUARREL
QUARRIES
QUARTERS
QUARTUS
QUATERNION
QUEEN
QUENCH
QUESTIONS

QUICK
QUICKENETH
QUICKLY
QUICKSANDS
QUIET
QUIETLY
QUIETNESS
QUIT
QUIVER
QUIVERED

```
Q Q U U Q U U S M S S K Q K Q
S Y R K S K R U Q E K U K U U
T L X X U E G N I K A U Q S I
T T Z Z T K K R S I Q U U S E
T E H R R K R S L S I S A E T
Q I A K A A S S S C S N R N T
U U U U U Q U K K Q U E R T O
Q Q S Q Q H U S K U K E E E I
U Q Q U U C A K K K K U L I N
I H H T E N E K C I U Q K U R
V Q Z Z D E Q I K U E M U Q E
E X X S S U U S R Q M K Q I T
R E V I U Q U I C K L Y A Q A
E Y U S N O I T S E U Q Q U U
D X R Q S R T B L T S M R Q Q
```

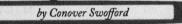

by Conover Swofford

66 ___

Visit of a Queen

1 Kings 10:1–13

APPAREL	LORD
BELIEVED	MEAT
BOUNTY	MEN
CAMELS	PRECIOUS STONES
CUPBEARERS	PROSPERITY
EXCEEDETH	QUEEN
FAME	REPORT
GOLD	SERVANTS
HARPS	SHEBA
ISRAEL	SOLOMON
JERUSALEM	SPICES
KING	WISDOM

S H S E S L T X Y S B A S I D
T A E M X Z E C S E H R M E N
Q R N G A C D R L E E E Y Y M
T R O P E R E I A R C T B X X
M I T Q O W E E A P N I A A P
O H S L Z V T E D U P V P X A
D E S Y E L B N O E W A J S L
S O U D G P C B M E T Y E J E
I P O I U C A M E L S H R N T
W S I C S T N A V R E S U O K
R F C Q B R F D N D P G S M S
Q U E E N A A N L R J N A O E
I U R L M O N E A O K I L L L
I C P E J R S H L B G K E O G
P R O S P E R I T Y H D M S Y

by Ruth Graether

67

R's in the Bible

RABBI
RACHEL
RAFTERS
RAMOTHGILEAD
REBEKAH
REBELLION
REBUKER
RECOMPENCE
REDEMPTION
REFUGE
REGENERATION
RELIGION
REMEMBRANCE

RENDER
REPENTANCE
REPHAIMS
REPROACH
REREWARD
RESPECT
RESTORE
RESURRECTION
REUEL
RICH
RINGLEADER
RINGSTRAKED

```
R  I  B  B  A  R  N  O  I  L  L  E  B  E  R
R  H  A  K  E  B  E  R  R  E  S  T  O  R  E
R  C  H  R  R  S  M  I  A  H  P  E  R  D  S
R  A  F  T  E  R  S  R  E  B  U  K  E  R  U
N  O  I  T  A  R  E  N  E  G  E  R  R  A  R
E  R  E  C  O  M  P  E  N  C  E  I  E  W  R
C  P  R  A  C  H  E  L  N  D  T  N  D  E  E
N  E  M  R  M  R  M  A  E  R  C  G  A  R  C
A  R  E  N  D  E  R  M  R  H  E  S  E  E  T
T  I  M  T  T  B  P  P  S  S  P  T  L  R  I
N  C  S  R  M  T  R  R  R  S  S  R  G  E  O
E  H  R  E  I  Z  X  X  Y  Z  E  A  N  F  N
P  R  M  O  I  S  L  E  U  E  R  K  I  U  S
E  E  N  R  R  N  O  I  G  I  L  E  R  G  P
R  A  M  O  T  H  G  I  L  E  A  D  H  E  S
```

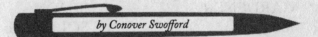

by Conover Swofford

In Jesus' parable of the ten virgins, why were five foolish women not prepared to enter the bridal party?

They took no extra oil for their lamps, and their lamps had gone out. (Matthew 25:1–8)

68

The Resurrection of Christ

ALIVE
BELIEVE
CLEOPAS
CLOTHES
DISCIPLES
EARTHQUAKE
EMMAUS
FATHER
GARDENER
ISRAEL
JESUS
LINEN
LORD
MARY MAGDALENE

MASTER
NAILS
PEACE
PETER
PRINT
PROPHETS
RISEN
SEPULCHRE
SIMON
SOLDIERS
STONE
THOMAS

```
M A S T E R Y Y J H U K E P S
R S Y W O N R L B I B J M R U
E S E S O L D I E R S C Z O A
T P S K H Z D R A D P O R P M
E N E L A D G A M Y R A M H M
P G Q I R U L N E B C L S E E
R Q A O S E Q R A L P N E T S
I N L R A A H H O I E S L S T
N O F R D C P T T S L V P L O
T M S A L E H O I R C S I B N
Q I K U T E N R E K A N C L E
I S P V S H W E Y L E E S W A
Z E V E I L E B R N C Q I G I
S A M O H T K R W J A U D Z D
E C A E P V R J E S U S B Z G
```

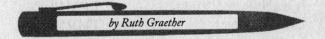

by Ruth Graether

69

The Book
of Revelation

ANGELS

BEAST

CANDLESTICK

CHURCH

DRAGON

EARTH

GLORY

HEAVEN

JOHN

LAMB

LIFE

LION

LOCUSTS

MARRIAGE

MICHAEL

OVERCOMETH

PARADISE

PILLAR

RAINBOW

RIVER

SATAN

SEALS

SEVEN

STAR

SUPPER

TEMPLE

THRONE

TREE

TRUMPET

VIAL

WITNESS

WOMAN

WORMWOOD

```
A B K Q S T S U C O L D D G B
Z Q L V I A L X X X Y R O L G
J M I C H A E L P M E T R E E
O A F C E R A I N B O W J O S
J R E N A N G E L S E A L S E
E R R E V I R R A E A J I O N
S I R R E N R R M V R Y O V O
I A A W N A A Q B E T Z N E R
D G L O J T J E F N H G G R H
A E L M S A A S U P P E R C T
R S I A U S S E N T I W S O S
A X P N T R U M P E T O O M H
P J H C R U H C S T S C R E L
N O G A R D O O W M R O W T H
J C A N D L E S T I C K O H J
```

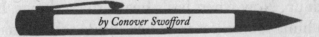

by Conover Swofford

⚡Bonus Trivia

According to Paul's message in Athens,
what assurance has God given us that
Christ will judge the world?

He raised Him from the dead. (Acts 17:16, 31)

70

The Rich Young Ruler

Luke 18:18–23

And a **certain ruler** asked him, saying, **Good Master**, what shall I do to **inherit eternal life**? And **Jesus** said unto him, Why **callest** thou me good? **none** is good, **save one**, that is, **God**. Thou **knowest** the **commandments**, Do not **commit adultery**, Do not **kill**, Do not **steal**, Do not **bear false witness**, **Honour** thy **father** and thy **mother**. And he said, All these have I **kept** from my **youth** up. Now when Jesus **heard** these things, he said unto him, Yet lackest thou one thing: **sell** all that thou hast, and **distribute** unto the **poor**, and thou shalt have **treasure** in **heaven**: and **come**, **follow** me. And when he heard this, he was **very sorrowful**: for he was very **rich**.

```
K E P T G O D R F N E V A E H
E T E R N A L S A V E I Q N R
Q A W O L L O F Z G O O D G U
I D E R E R A E B H E A R D L
K U M S E T U B I R T S I D E
N L O Y R E V E W F A T H E R
O T C V O H R I C A L L E S T
W E A L O U T I R E H N I M L
E R R N S N T M F M O T H E R
S Y O A E I A H C E R T A I N
T U E S M S T E A L R O O P E
R R S M T H E S L A F G P X N
T L O E C S O R R O W F U L O
A C R I J L I F E L L I K P N
Y X R C O M M A N D M E N T S
```

by N. Teri Grottke

S's in the Bible

SABBATH
SACKCLOTH
SACRIFICES
SALUTATION
SALVATION
SANCTUARY
SAPPHIRA
SATISFACTION
SAVIOUR
SAVOUR
SCAPEGOAT
SCARLET
SCORPIONS
SCRIBES

SCRIPTURE
SELAH
SELLER
SERAPHIMS
SHERIFFS
SHIBBOLETH
SILVERSMITH
SINGING
SISERA
SISTER
STOREHOUSE
SYNAGOGUE
SYNTYCHE

```
S S E L A H T E L O B B I H S S
A S A P P H I R A S T H S A A S
L H S B E H C Y T N Y S L S T S
V T A Y B A R E S I S U E C I S
A I C R S A S T T R T E S A S E
T M R A A Z T X X A U T S R F R
I S I U V Q U H T D R M T L A U
O R F T O S S I D R S S T E C T
N E I C U S O A C C D F S T T P
S V C N R N S H E R I F F S I I
E L E A C E U G O G A N Y S O R
L I S S C A P E G O A T X X N C
L S M I H P A R E S C R I B E S
E S U O H E R O T S I S T E R X
R U O I V A S A C K C L O T H X
X G N I G N I S N O I P R O C S
```

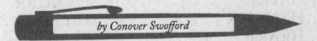

by Conover Swofford

⚡Bonus Trivia

In Ephesians, why did Paul tell us
salvation could not be accomplished
by "works"?

Lest men should boast. (Ephesians 2:8–9)

72

Song of Deborah

Judges 5:2–31

ARCHERS
AWAKE
BENJAMIN
BREACHES
DEBORAH
DISH
FLOCKS
GATES
HAMMER
HEART
HEBER
HORSEHOOFS
JAEL
KINGS
KISHON

LIVES
LORD
MEROZ
MIGHTY
MOUNTAINS
PRAISE
REUBEN
SHAMGAR
SHIELD
SINAI
SISERA
SPEAK
SPEAR
SUN

```
B F N R B C M O U N T A I N S
L G I U A S K L V F L O C K S
E H M S S F J K I N G S F L Q
S I A K P O S M S N Z E E P L
Q J J A E O R S H I E L D O O
E D N V A H E E A K N B G N R
K I E M R E H H M I A D U M D
A S B X Z S C C G S R T H E R
E H Q G I R R A A H E R I R R
P K P A R O A E R O M A J O S
S L N T E H I R W N M E L Z J
D I O E B D E B O R A H I M A
S S I S E R A T X Y H C V L E
B M N Y H M I G H T Y B E K L
A A W A K E H U P R A I S E U
```

by Angela Fletcher

⚡Bonus Trivia

What was the answer to Samson's riddle, "Out of the eater came forth meat, and out of the strong came forth sweetness"?

Honey from a lion's carcass. (Judges 14:12–18)

73

Song of Moses

Exodus 15:1–18

ARM	RED SEA
BLOW	REIGN
EARTH	RIGHT HAND
ENEMY	SALVATION
EXALT	SEA
GLORIOUSLY	SING
GREATNESS	SONG
HORSE	SPOIL
LORD	STONE
MAN OF WAR	STRENGTH
MERCY	STUBBLE
MY GOD	THEE
OVERTHROWN	TRIUMPHED
PHARAOH'S	WATERS
POWER	WRATH
PURSUE	

```
S I N G H G P H A R A O H S A
A P T H E E C S E A V T O I L
B U M Y G O D B W X R E V W C
G R E A T N E S S A A R E H M
L S S T U B B L E R U L R H E
O U Y C R E M O Y E B L T R S
R E G L A R M R X D T G H A R
I C P N J A E D Z S N M R W O
O Y Q E O B L O W E C R O F H
U W R N K S F W R A T H W O E
S A P O W E R T R E I G N N S
L W A T E R S A E N E M Y A P
Y V S S A L V A T I O N R M O
C R I G H T H A N D S O Q G I
D U T T R I U M P H E D P F L
```

by Angela Fletcher

74

T's in the Bible

TABBAOTH
TABLETS
TARSUS
TATTLERS
TEKEL
TEMPERANCE
TEMPTATION
TESTAMENT
THANKSGIVING
THE TWELVE
THEATRE
THIGH
THISTLES

THORNS
THREESCORE
THRESHING
TITHES
TOKEN
TONGUES
TOOTH
TORMENTED
TOSSINGS
TRANSGRESSION
TREASURES
TRESPASSES
TRUTH

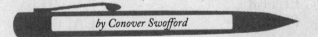

```
T  T  R  U  T  H  R  E  E  S  C  O  R  E  T
T  R  T  T  E  I  D  E  T  N  E  M  R  O  T
X  A  N  E  K  O  T  X  S  R  T  T  T  H  S
T  N  S  M  E  T  H  H  T  R  S  S  I  S  G
X  S  E  P  L  E  E  S  E  S  S  G  N  G  N
N  G  S  E  T  S  T  R  L  S  H  R  T  N  I
O  R  S  R  O  T  W  S  B  H  O  M  T  I  V
I  E  A  A  S  A  E  S  A  H  H  N  T  H  I
T  S  P  N  S  M  L  S  T  A  R  S  U  S  G
A  S  S  C  I  E  V  T  H  I  S  T  L  E  S
T  I  E  E  N  N  E  H  T  O  O  T  H  R  K
P  O  R  M  G  T  A  T  T  L  E  R  S  H  N
M  N  T  M  S  E  U  G  N  O  T  M  M  T  A
E  S  T  T  T  S  E  R  U  S  A  E  R  T  H
T  H  E  A  T  R  E  H  T  O  A  B  B  A  T
```

by Conover Swofford

Bonus Trivia

Who said, "What have I done unto thee, that thou hast smitten me these three times?"

Balaam's donkey. (Numbers 22:28)

75

Twelves

APOSTLES:

ANDREW
BARTHOLOMEW
JAMES
JAMES [SON OF
    ALPHAEUS]
JOHN
MATTHEW
MATTHIAS
PETER
PHILIP
SIMON
THADDAEUS
THOMAS

TRIBES:

ASHER
BENJAMIN
DAN
EPHRAIM
GAD
ISSACHAR
JUDAH
MANASSEH
NAPHTALI
REUBEN
SIMEON
ZEBULUN

SPIES:

AMMIEL
CALEB
GADDI
GADDIEL
GEUEL
IGAL
NAHBI
OSHEA
PALTI
SETHUR
SHAMMUA
SHAPHAT

```
P A L T I S S A C H A R H A I G
H J S I M H A D U J N A P M N E
I I S S A H E S S A N A M A O U
L C A L E B W L N M W J N T E E
I N E B U E R U S E E O A T M L
P A D D R D L D M S H H H H I H
N I J D S U H O D D T N B I S M
I L N N B R L G A D T O I A M U
M A Z E E O Z A Z J A M E S I E
A T Z T H G Z D A N M I R Z A R
J H E T H A D D A E U S E X R U
N P R H E D U I S A M O H T H H
E A M A N D A E G A E H S O P T
B N L A G I U L E I M M A R E E
S H A P H A T P H A U M M A H S
A H J Z E B M A N I S A A B R M
```

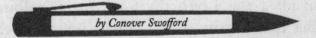

by Conover Swofford

76

The Ten Commandments

Exodus 20:3–8, 10, 12–17

Thou shalt have no **other gods** before me. Thou shalt not make unto thee any **graven image**, or any **likeness** of any thing that is in **heaven** above, or that is in the **earth** beneath, or that is in the **water** under the earth. Thou shalt not **bow down** thyself to them, nor **serve** them: for I the LORD thy God am a **jealous** God, visiting the iniquity of the fathers upon the children unto the third and fourth **generation** of them that hate me; and showing **mercy** unto **thousands** of them that love me, and keep my **commandments**. Thou shalt not take the **name** of the LORD thy God in **vain**. . . . Remember the **sabbath** day, to keep it **holy**. . . . The **seventh day** is the sabbath of the LORD thy God: in it thou shalt not do any work, thou, nor thy son, nor thy daughter, thy manservant, nor thy **maidservant**. . . . **Honour** thy **father** and thy **mother**. . . . Thou **shalt not** kill. Thou shalt not commit **adultery**. Thou shalt not **steal**. Thou shalt not bear **false witness** against thy neighbour. Thou shalt not **covet**. . . .

```
C M M S S E N T I W E S L A F
M O C C N I A V C E M A N M M
M M Y R E T L U D A S S H T D
M A I D S E R V A N T T T T T
F A T H E R W A T E R E O S T
O T H E R G O D S A A A N U N
H L O H H E A V E N I L T O O
M L U H M T R M F L T H L L I
E I S T A W M N I R O O A A T
R K A A O H W K H N M L H E A
C E N B H O E H O N E Y S J R
Y V D B D N M U M T E V O C E
R R S A E R R E H T O M A H N
R E R S E V E N T H D A Y R E
R S S T N E M D N A M M O C G
```

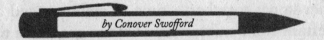

by Conover Swofford

⚡Bonus Trivia

In God's perfect kingdom, the wolf will
dwell with what?

77

A Time for All Seasons

Ecclesiastes 3:1–8

To every thing there is a **season,** and a time to every purpose under the **heaven:** a time to be **born,** and a time to **die;** a time to **plant,** and a time to **pluck** up that which is planted; a time to **kill,** and a time to **heal;** a time to break **down,** and a time to **build** up; a time to **weep,** and a time to **laugh;** a time to **mourn,** and a time to **dance;** a time to cast away **stones,** and a time to **gather** stones together; a time to **embrace,** and a time to **refrain** from embracing; a time to **get,** and a time to **lose;** a time to **keep,** and a time to cast **away;** a time to **rend,** and a time to **sew;** a time to keep **silence,** and a time to **speak;** a time to **love,** and a time to **hate;** a time of **war,** and a time of **peace.**

```
L H P E Q D S R T I P A D N C
M A L V M E F W Z E B E W R O
B T A R N B S N J V G R A A N
R E N O W P R N O S A E S C Y
L E T J E O K A M W H K P M E
O S H A B E G A C R G E I D X
V G K T E E S W S E U W X L H
E N M P A I Q K D F A T K L L
E S O L L G J O T R L A Y C N
W E B E N D W G D A N C E R D
E J N P E N L Y J I P L U C K
S C T E V F Q I R N S O K C M
E R I E A H L Q U A M H E A L
G G N W E V Q O O B E D V X B
H T I M H E S D N E R Y S S P
```

by Ruth Graether

⚡Bonus Trivia

What did a voice from heaven instruct hungry Peter to do after he fell into a trance?

"Rise, Peter; kill, and eat." (Acts 10:9–13)

78

U's in the Bible

UNBELIEVING
UNCLE
UNCORRUPTNESS
UNDERNEATH
UNDERSTANDING
UNKNOWN GOD
UNPROFITABLE
UNREASONABLE
UNRULY
UNSPOTTED
UNSTABLE
UPHARSIN

UPPER
UPROAR
URBANE
URGE
URIAH
USURP
USURY
UTHAI
UTTERED
UTTERMOST
UZZIAH
UZZIEL

```
V V H A I Z Z U X V V U R G E
V Y L U R N U N H H H N T U U
U N C O R R U P T N E S S N U
N Y R U S U S R P L U P O D E
D S R U U I U O H E H O M E L
E L C N U T R F X I R T R R B
R S T S R T P I X Z Z T E N A
S U R B A N E T Z Z Z E T E N
T R A O R P U A Z U U D T A O
A Z Z U Z Z U B H A I R U T S
N G N I V E I L E B N U U H A
D M N H Z U D E R E T T U H E
I M N H U Z E L B A T S N U R
N I S R A H P U T H A I H H N
G H U Z Z D O G N W O N K N U
```

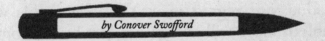

by Conover Swofford

How did God evaluate His work after six
days of creative labor?

79

The Unjust Judge

Luke 18:1-8

And he spake a parable unto them to this end, that men ought always to pray, and not to faint; Saying, There was in a **city** a **judge**, which **feared** not **God**, **neither regarded man**: And there was a **widow** in that city; and she came unto him, **saying**, Avenge me of **mine adversary**. And he would not for a while: but **afterward** he said **within himself**, Though I **fear** not God, **nor regard** man; Yet because this widow **troubleth** me, I will avenge her, **lest** by her continual **coming** she **weary** me. And the **Lord** said, **Hear** what the **unjust** judge **saith**. And **shall** not God avenge his **own elect**, which **cry day** and **night** unto him, though he **bear long** with them? I tell you that he will **avenge** them **speedily. Nevertheless** when the **Son** of man cometh, shall he **find faith** on the **earth**?

```
K L G N E I T H E R S H A L L
W I D O W D N I F N I H T I W
U R K R D F T R O U B L E T H
D E D R A G E R C O M I N G Q
T G R C N E E N O S S A I T H
S A O O R G F S P C W E A R Y
U R L C N Y R A S R E V D A P
J D I E G N I Y A S T B E A R
N E V E R T H E L E S S R P H
U A N L N N A F T E R W A R D
K W P E A I E W N L P H E A R
O I H C E G M I H T I A F N Y
L E S T D Y G S P E E D I L Y
M A N U A H I M S E L F B U C
Y F J D T W C I T Y H T R A E
```

by N. Teri Grottke

Bonus Trivia

What charge was made by false witnesses against Jesus before Caiaphas, the high priest?

80

V's in the Bible

VAGABOND	VILLAGES
VALIANT	VINE
VANISH	VINEGAR
VANITY	VINEYARD
VASHTI	VINTAGE
VEHEMENTLY	VIOLENCE
VENGEANCE	VIRGIN
VENTURE	VIRTUOUS
VERILY	VISAGE
VERMILION	VOICE
VESSELS	VOID
VESTMENTS	VOLUME
VEXATION	VOW
VICTUALS	VOYAGE

```
S T N E M T S E V I T H S A V
V O I C E Y L T N E M E H E V
E H V V S U O U T R I V N D I
R S S L E S S E V I R G I N N
M I V E N T U R E V E O V M E
I N V D N O B A G A V I N E Y
L A V V A L I A N T V V X Y A
I V I O V V I C T U A L S A R
O I S W I V E X A T I O N R D
N O A Z N X V I L L A G E S V
G L G Z E V X V X Y L I R E V
V E E E G A T N I V A N I T Y
Y N V V A Z X V V Y R S S M M
V C X X R V M N D C M E V X X
V E G A Y O V O L U M E V X X
```

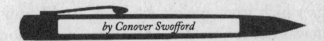

by Conover Swofford

How did the believers react to Saul
when he returned to Jerusalem after his
conversion?

They were afraid of him. (Acts 9:22, 26)

81

The Voyage Begins

Acts 27:9–13

Now when much **time** was spent, and when **sailing** was now **dangerous**, because the **fast** was now **already past**, Paul **admonished** them, and said unto them, **Sirs**, I **perceive** that this **voyage** will be with **hurt** and **much damage**, not **only** of the lading and **ship**, but also of our **lives**. **Nevertheless** the **centurion believed** the **master** and the **owner** of the ship, more than those things which were **spoken** by **Paul**. And because the haven was not commodious to winter in, the more part advised to **depart** thence also, if by any **means** they might **attain** to **Phenice**, and there to winter; which is an **haven** of **Crete**, and **lieth toward** the **south west** and **north** west. And when the south wind **blew** softly, **supposing** that they had obtained their **purpose**, loosing thence, they sailed close by Crete.

```
H C U M A E S O P R U P I H S
T G N I S O P P U S N H S S Y
D F A Y C E G A Y O V E I A I
E V I E C R E P I N G N R D D
V H O N L Y E R S E D I S M A
E T I M E A U T L V R C A O N
I R L H T T S U E E A E I N G
L O W T N E A E Q R W H L I E
E N A E V P G L E T O U I S R
B I C I S A O T R H T R N H O
N W L L M T S W D E T T G E U
N E V A H A F D N L A U S D S
C L D F M S P O K E N D O A K
B B M E A N S A F S R X Y S P
R J A D E P A R T S A F C M X
```

by N. Teri Grottke

82

Biblical Valleys

ACHOR
AJALON
BERACHAH
CHARASHIM
CRAFTSMEN
DECISION
ELAH
ESCHOL
GERAR
GIANTS
GIBEON
HAMONGOG
HEBRON
HINNOM
JERICHO
JEZREEL

JIPHTHAHEL
KEZIZ
KINGS
MEGIDDO
MIZPEH
MOUNTAINS
PASSENGERS
SALT
SHITTIM
SLAUGHTER
SOREK
VISION
ZARED
ZEBOIM
ZEPHATHAH

```
O H P Z H E P Z I M I O B E Z
H H I N N O M Z O D D I G E M
Z P C S R E G N E S S A P N O
J J M I T T I H S J S H O S U
Z H E B R O N P H A A L G J N
H H S O R E K J L T A N R Z T
A D E R A Z J T H J I J L L A
M M M R O H C A A K J K Z L I
O M H A L E H A H T H P I J N
N E M S T F A R C Z I Z E K S
G Z R E T H G U A L S L L T J
O P E M I H S A R A H C N Z K
G H N O I S I C E D R A R E G
M I L O H C S E B V I S I O N
J J E Z R E E L J G I B E O N
```

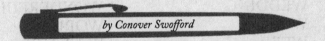

by Conover Swofford

83

W's in the Bible

WAFERS
WAGES
WAIT
WALK
WALLOW
WATERS
WAX
WAY
WEALTH
WEARINESS
WEDDING
WEDGE
WEEP

WIDOW
WIFE
WILD
WILLOWS
WIMPLES
WINE
WINKED
WINNOWED
WISDOM
WISE MEN
WONDERFUL
WORD
WORSHIP

```
W M X Z M O D S I W E D G E W
A A H H S R E F A W R S P E A
L K I K L A W A T E R S E W Y
L H N T M Z O X X N P P X A W
O H M I N R N U Z M P P W W O
W O D I W O N D E R F U L W R
I W D M E D I R M W W I L D D
L W E W A S W E D D I N G W H
L D K E R T O W W Z S X X W W
O H N M I T R F Z Z E X X I H
W W I W N S S D C F M W W F W
S H W H E E H D C M E M W E W
T H H S S N I H R R N H R R R
W A G E S I P R S E L P M I W
W N M N M W E A L T H S T T W
```

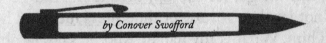

by Conover Swofford

Bonus Trivia

What were Jesus' final words before His death?

"Father, into thy hands I commend my spirit." (Luke 23:46)

84

Wrestling with God

Genesis 32:22–32

And he **rose** up that **night**, and took his two wives, and his two womenservants, and his **eleven** sons, and passed over the ford **Jabbok**. And he took them, and sent them over the **brook**, and sent over that he had. And **Jacob** was left alone; and there **wrestled** a man with him until the breaking of the **day**. And when he saw that he **prevailed** not against him, he touched the **hollow** of his **thigh**; and the hollow of Jacob's thigh was out of **joint**, as he wrestled with him. And he said, Let me go, for the **day breaketh**. And he said, I will not let thee go, except thou **bless me**. And he said unto him, What is thy name? And he said, Jacob. And he said, Thy name shall be **called** no more Jacob, but **Israel**: for as a **prince** hast thou **power** with **God** and with men, and hast **prevailed**. And Jacob asked him, and said, Tell me, I pray thee, thy name. And he said, Wherefore is it that thou dost ask after my name? And he blessed him there. And Jacob called the name of the place **Peniel**: for I have seen God **face to face**, and my life is preserved. And as he passed over **Penuel** the **sun** rose upon him, and he **halted** upon his thigh. Therefore the children of Israel eat not of the **sinew** which shrank, which is upon the hollow of the thigh, unto this day: because he touched the hollow of Jacob's thigh in the sinew that shrank.

J	T	H	G	F	E	D	J	A	C	O	B	C	B	A
A	H	L	D	A	Y	B	R	E	A	K	E	T	H	O
R	G	W	L	V	H	J	T	C	R	Q	H	I	P	P
O	I	Z	E	A	O	B	D	A	D	S	F	R	R	J
S	N	M	U	I	L	D	A	F	D	I	I	D	E	A
E	O	P	N	Q	L	E	Y	O	E	N	U	E	V	B
B	A	T	E	Z	O	L	P	T	L	E	V	L	A	B
L	I	M	P	E	W	L	O	E	I	W	E	T	I	O
H	B	R	O	O	K	A	W	C	A	G	F	S	L	K
A	U	N	J	T	L	C	E	A	V	N	N	E	E	O
L	E	C	N	I	R	P	R	F	E	P	Q	R	D	P
T	H	G	I	H	T	T	Z	V	R	A	B	W	C	D
E	L	S	U	N	H	S	E	I	P	F	G	O	D	E
D	I	S	R	A	E	L	G	P	E	N	I	E	L	P
W	R	E	S	T	E	C	Q	B	L	E	S	S	M	E

by Angela Fletcher

⚡Bonus Trivia

What did David win by defeating
Goliath?

85

Biblical Weights, Measures, and Monies

BATH	LENGTH
BEKAH	LOG
CAB	MANEH
COR	MILE
CUBIT	MITE
DRAM	OMER
EPHAH	PENCE
FARTHING	PENNY
FURLONG	ROD
GERAH	SHEKEL
GOLD	SILVER
HANDBREADTH	TALENT
HIN	

```
R E G G A L R U F U T I C H T
H G A T H A T I E L S K O R D
I Q M A N E H N A I H T N R I
N Z K L X X X R B A T H A E S
A E A E C U B I T P T M H P H
B T C N O A O N N D E G P H E
I I M T C I D O A P I N R A K
P M I A S O O E I L L I C H E
E M L Y M N R E M O Y H T E L
N Z E Y Z B Z N M R K T R H E
N S T A D R E V L I S R I P L
Y T M N C H T G N E L A T A L
M A A R O G E L O G E F E E R
I H A R E G E G S T T A M O R
N F U R L O N G D L O G R U G
```

by Conover Swofford

86

Cleansing the Way

Psalm 119:9–16

Wherewithal shall a **young man** cleanse his way? by **taking heed thereto according** to thy **word**. With my **whole heart** have I **sought** thee: O **let** me not **wander** from thy **commandments**. Thy word have I **hid** in **mine** heart, that I **might** not **sin against** thee. Blessed **art** thou, O LORD: **teach** me thy statutes. With my **lips** have I **declared all** the **judgments** of thy **mouth**. I have **rejoiced** in the **way** of thy **testimonies**, as **much** as in all **riches**. I will **meditate** in thy **precepts**, and have **respect** unto thy ways. I will **delight** myself in thy statutes: I will not **forget** thy word.

```
H M T A L T S S O U G H T S T
I U E G Q A H E L I P S T T H
D C G A H W H G H U F N E N G
E H R I T T A T I C E L T E I
C R O N A E U N I M I O A M L
L E F S K S T O D W B R T G E
A J A T I T E N M E E D I D D
R O L V N I A M A N R R D U Y
E I L L G M C R V A R T E J A
D C E P M O H A M I N E M H W
Q E T O G N R E S P E C T C W
Q D C G S I N H Q G N U O Y H
T R A E H E M T H E R E T O O
H D R O W S S T P E C E R P L
T A C C O R D I N G D E E H E
```

by N. Teri Grottke

87

Y's and Z's in the Bible

YEA	ZAZA
YEAR	ZEALOUSLY
YEARN	ZELOPHEHAD
YELLOW	ZENAS
YESTERDAY	ZEPHONITES
YET	ZERUAH
YIELDING	ZIF
YOKE	ZION
YONDER	ZIPH
YOU	ZIPHRON
YOUNG	ZOAN
YOURSELVES	ZOAR
YOUTH	ZUPH

```
Z I P H R O N N R A E Y O K E
Z I Y G Z Y Z Y E Z A E Z Z Z
Z Z O N Z R Y Y X D X L Y Y E
M Z Z I F R A R R R R L S T R
Z M E D Z R R E R R R O M C U
H S L L Y Z T E Y Y E W Z Z A
H E O E X S D S T N A O Z X H
T T P I E N Y Z Z E Y M E Y A
U I H Y O U R S E L V E S Z Z
O N E Y O U N G S H Z S H S A
Y O H S S U Y L S U O L A E Z
Y H A S S O S R T R A R M E H
O P D S S Y T H Z E R E N M R
Y E M H P U Z A A A Y A A D T
Z Z C D C D H P I Z S N O I Z
```

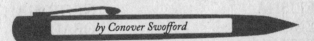

by Conover Swofford

In what room of the first temple was the
ark of the covenant kept?

The most holy place. (1 Kings 8:6)

88

God Is Faithful in the Old Testament

AARON
ABEDNEGO
AMRAM
BARAK
CALEB
DANIEL
DEBORAH
ELIJAH
ELISHA
ENOCH
ESTHER
EZRA
HEBREW MIDWIVES
HEZEKIAH
ISAIAH
JACOB

JEREMIAH
JOB
JOCHEBED
JOSEPH
JOSHUA
MESHACH
MORDECAI
MOSES
NEHEMIAH
OBADIAH
OTHNIEL
RAHAB
SARAH
SHADRACH
ZEPHANIAH

```
D A N I E L O H A I M E H E N
S N L H A I N A H P E Z R A S
E R H A R O B E D S A R A H H
V H E I Z S A E L I S H A C A
I A Z A M A R M A K M D E O U
W J E S E C A A B B R B B N H
D I K I N S K K J A C O B E S
I L I M O R D E C A I B B O O
M E A L C A B H A I M E R E J
W I H A H A H A C H L L L S O
E N T C H H R I R A H A B T S
R H H A C O R D C N H T T H E
B T R R N A T A H A H S S E P
E O G E N D E B A S S S E R H
H D E B E H C O J S E S O M M
```

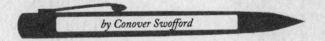

by Conover Swofford

🗲 Bonus Trivia

According to Ephesians, what is the
Christian's shield that equips him to
"quench all the fiery darts of the wicked"?

The shield of faith. (Ephesians 6:16)

89

God Is Faithful in the New Testament

ANANIAS
BARNABAS
CORNELIUS
DORCAS
ELISABETH
EUNICE
JOSEPH [OF
    ARIMATHAEA]
LAZARUS
LOIS
LYDIA
MARTHA
MARY
NICANOR
NICODEMUS

NICOLAS
ONESIMUS
PARMENAS
PAUL
PHEBE
PHILIP
PROCHORUS
SILAS
STEPHEN
TABITHA
TIMON
TIMOTHEUS
TITUS
WITNESS
ZACCHAEUS

```
T I M O T H E U S A I D Y L O
I A P I L I H P R O N A C I N
M H B P A R M E N A S O M I E
O T S I M N E H P E T S C M S
N R A O T A C H O S A O O A I
I A B E J H T H I L D A M R M
C M A C M O A L S E M A K Y U
O I N I S E A U M D O R C A S
L P R N T S E U K L U A P J U
A S A U H A S S E N T I W O R
S E B E H P R O C H O R U S A
S H M C O H T E B A S I L E Z
H M C X O S L O I S W S S P A
S A N A N I A S U T I T W H L
Z T O L T S S U I L E N R O C
```

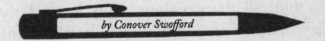

by Conover Swofford

⚡Bonus Trivia

What did Jeremiah, Daniel, and Isaiah
have in common?

They were prophets.

90

Save, Lord

Psalm 20

The LORD **hear** thee in the day of **trouble**; the name of the God of Jacob **defend** thee; send thee help from the **sanctuary**, and strengthen thee out of **Zion**; remember all thy **offerings**, and accept thy burnt **sacrifice**; Selah. Grant thee according to thine own **heart**, and fulfil all thy **counsel**. We will **rejoice** in thy **salvation**, and in the name of our God we will set up our banners: the LORD fulfil all thy **petitions**. Now know I that the LORD saveth his **anointed**; he will hear him from his holy **heaven** with the saving strength of his right hand. Some **trust** in chariots, and some in horses: but we will remember the **name** of the LORD our God. They are **brought down** and fallen: but we are **risen**, and stand upright. **Save**, LORD: let the **king** hear us when we **call**.

```
A  N  A  M  E  B  T  R  O  U  B  L  E  C  D
S  A  L  V  A  T  I  O  N  E  F  L  G  T  H
A  A  L  E  S  N  U  O  C  E  J  A  K  R  L
N  B  V  N  R  P  Q  V  S  G  A  C  U  U  V
C  R  X  E  O  F  F  E  R  I  N  G  S  S  Y
T  O  Z  A  B  K  I  N  G  C  O  D  A  T  D
U  U  E  F  H  G  J  I  P  K  I  L  C  M  N
A  G  N  D  E  S  I  R  E  O  N  P  R  Q  E
R  H  R  S  A  T  R  E  V  D  T  W  I  X  F
Y  T  Y  Z  V  A  A  J  R  B  E  C  F  D  E
T  D  F  G  E  H  I  O  J  K  D  L  I  M  D
R  O  O  H  N  P  L  I  Q  B  S  T  C  F  V
A  W  S  X  O  Z  A  C  N  X  D  E  E  W  G
E  N  I  L  K  L  P  E  T  I  T  I  O  N  S
H  M  R  I  S  E  N  N  O  P  Z  I  O  N  Q
```

by Angela Fletcher

91

Paul's Missionary Journeys

ANTIOCH
ATHENS
ATTALIA
BEREA
CAESAREA
CENCHREA
CNIDUS
CRETE
DAMASCUS
DERBE
EPHESUS
GALATIA
JERUSALEM
LYSTRA

MACEDONIA
MELITA
MILETUS
NEAPOLIS
PATARA
PHRYGIA
RHEGIUM
ROME
SAMOTHRACIA
SIDON
THESSALONICA
THYATIRA
TROAS
TYRE

```
N O D I S T B B E R E A M D A
B X T E S N E H T A E I E A R
M P Y M E L I T A R S L L M T
A R I T A Y H T Y S B A A A S
G A L A T I A T U U R T S S Y
A C I N O L A S S E H T U C L
O C I C C A E S A R E A R U D
M S E Y A H H I U N S H E S E
Y I X N P R N C E D E A J P R
C I L E C O H A O G I A O H B
E R L E D H P T I I R N M R E
M Q E E T O R U O A T A C Y T
O B C T L U M E T M Q N V G B
R A M I E B S A A T A I A I J
M Q S Z U I P T A T K S C A V
```

by Ruth Graether

⚡Bonus Trivia

What did Paul tell Timothy was the
root of all kinds of evil?

"The love of money." (1 Timothy 6:10)

92

Paul's Testimony Before King Agrippa

Acts 25:12–26:31

ACCUSED	JERUSALEM
AGRIPPA	JESUS
ANSWER	JEWS
APPEALED	KING
AUTHORITY	MOSES
BLASPHEME	NAZARETH
BONDS	PAUL
CHRISTIAN	PERSECUTED
CUSTOMS	PRIESTS
DAMASCUS	PRISONER
DEAD	PROMISE
FESTUS	REPENT
FORGIVENESS	SANCTIFIED
GENTILES	SYNAGOGUE
GOD	TESTIFY
HOPE	

by Ruth Graether

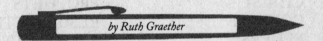

⚡Bonus Trivia

What did James advise those
lacking wisdom to do?

"Ask of God." (James 1:5)

93

Paul's Trial Before Felix and Festus

Acts 23:29–25:8

ACCUSE
ANANIAS
CAESAREA
CAPTAIN
CHARGE
CHRIST
COUNCIL
ELDERS
EVIL
FELIX
HIGH PRIEST
JERUSALEM
JEWS

LAW
LIBERTY
NATION
NAZARENES
PAUL
PROPHETS
RESURRECTION
RIGHTEOUSNESS
SYNAGOGUES
TEMPLE
THANKFULNESS
WORSHIP

W O R S H I P Y J W N S N L C
V E E D Y T R E B I L S A A H
K C N S R E R T A U O E Z W A
B E H J U U S T A Z Y N A K R
F S L R S C P P T P O L R Q G
A R Y A I A C C F I S U E A E
T N L N C S O A T A R F N E S
E E A C A U T C E N E K E R W
M V B N N G E E O P D N S A E
P D I C I R O I H G L A U S J
L U I L R A T G U P E H U E X
E L T U D A S Z U S O T G A B
Q H S R N N X I L E F R H C L
F E H I G H P R I E S T P I U
R S S E N S U O E T H G I R S

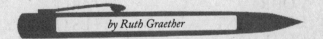

by Ruth Graether

⚡Bonus Trivia

When Jesus died on the cross, what was torn in two?

The veil of the temple. (Matthew 27:50-51)

94

The Tabernacle

AHOLIAB
ALMONDS
ALTAR
ARK
BEZALEEL
BRANCHES
BRASS
CANDLESTICK
CHERUBIMS
CONGREGATION
COURT
COVENANT
CURTAINS
FLOWERS

GOLD
HORNS
INCENSE
KNOPS
LAVER
OFFERING
OLIVE OIL
PURPLE
SHEWBREAD
STAVES
TABLE
TESTIMONY
VAIL

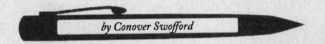

by Conover Swofford

Bonus Trivia

Who was turned into a pillar of salt for looking back at the destruction of a wicked city?

Lot's wife. (Genesis 19:23–26)

95

Sacrifices, Feasts, and Holy Days

SACRIFICES:

BURNT
   OFFERING
DRINK
MEAT
PEACE
SIN
TURTLEDOVES
WAVE
WOOD

FEASTS AND HOLY DAYS:

BOOTHS
CONVOCATIONS
DAY OF
   ATONEMENT
FEASTS [OF THE]
   LORD
FIRSTFRUITS
HARVEST
HOLY
INGATHERING
JEALOUSY
JUBILE
MEMORIAL
PASSOVER
PENTECOST
PURIM
SABBATH
UNLEAVENED
   BREAD

```
D A Y O F A T O N E M E N T T
L A I R O M E M E M Y L O H U
T S E V R A H T A B B A S G R
S L S R E V O S S A P P N N T
O O T J B O O T H S S I H I L
C R W E O D O O W R R S E R E
E D A A O R E T T E S H C E D
T S V L H I R N F M A A A H O
N T E O T N F F E A A A E T V
E S R U S K O S E V V V P A E
P A H S R T T T T A E M G S
U E M Y N J U B I L E E N N S
R F I R S T F R U I T S L I S
I R U C O N V O C A T I O N S
M B C N O O S I N I T N O N U
```

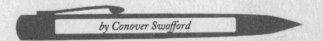

by Conover Swofford

⚡Bonus Trivia

Why did people go to the pool of
Bethesda?

To be healed. (John 5:1–4)

96

Clean and Unclean Animals

CLEAN ANIMALS:

CHAMOIS
GOAT
GRASSHOPPER
HART
LAMB
LOCUST
OX
PYGARG
ROEBUCK
SHEEP

UNCLEAN ANIMALS:

BAT
CAMEL
CONEY
CUCKOW
EAGLE
HARE
HAWK
HERON
KITE
OSPRAY
OWL
PELICAN
RAVEN
STORK
SWINE
VULTURE

```
B G H T Y Z X W X K J M M P N
E A T J K M Z Y Y Y Y Q R S S
V U L T U R E E L G A E P R G
A H E S H E E P Y G A R G R T
R R M C B A T L L U S S P T A
E L A M B G R W N X S W R S R
P O C R O X O T Y Z O Y E Y O
P C H A R E E H C K G M N M M
O U T X A Y B Z C X Y Z I X N
H S T T V H U U K K L M W P A
S T H J E K C H A M O I S P C
S A R R N I K O S S U Q Q I
A R O C H R I T N T H A W K L
R N Q X Z Y T X Z E X O O P E
G K R O T S E Y Y Y Y Z Z Z P
```

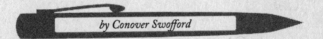

by Conover Swofford

97

Biblical Personalities

ABIGAIL
ADAM
AQUILA
DANIEL
DAVID
HEROD
JAMES
JEREMIAH
JESSE
JOHN
JOSEPH
LUKE
MAHLON
MARTHA
MARY
MATTHEW
MOSES

NAOMI
NOAH
PETER
PHEBE
PHILIP
PRISCILLA
RAHAB
RUTH
SAMUEL
SAUL
SIMEON
SOLOMON
TIMOTHY
TITUS
ZACCHAEUS
ZECHARIAH

```
Y N S J Z H N E M M E W A Y M
E T O S O O E R E R A B Y H A
L Z O M E S Z R A B I R L T H
E V E M O P E L O G E Y Y O L
U P I C J L L P A D R H N M O
M S F E H I O I H E F M P I N
A R S R C A L S T V A A J T O
S S U S L C R E P R Z D A J A
E T I I B H P I T P J A M E H
H R U Z A C C H A E U S E R Y
P Q L U K E A R A H A B S E I
A D A V I D A N I E L Q N M M
W E H T T A M P I L I H P I O
S E S O M S U T I T O Q E A A
L U A S W F H K B J G Q F H N
```

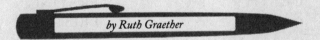

by Ruth Graether

⚡ Bonus Trivia

In the parable of the Good Samaritan, what condition was the traveler in when the thieves left him?

Naked and half dead. (Luke 10:30)

98

Peter's Escape from Prison

Acts 12:1–19

ANGEL
APPREHENDED
ASTONISHED
CHAINS
CHURCH
DEATH
EASTER
EXAMINED
GARMENT
HEROD
IRON GATE
JAMES
JOHN

KEEPERS
KNOCKED
LIGHT
MARY
PETER
PRAYING
PRISON
RHODA
SANDALS
SLEEPING
SOLDIERS
SOUGHT
UNLEAVENED

```
T S S P M K I E N C D D L D S
C L C R X Z F P X L U E E S O
D E D N E H E R P P A N N L L
D S L E E P I N G Q I E H A D
I E Y R A M E C O M H V G D I
E R H O D A H E A L D A R N E
E Z O S O A C X K E R E M A R
S A K N I Y E F K M T L N S S
O O S N G N B C E E I N N E Q
U L S T O A O N P C H U R C H
G D E S E N T T G N I Y A R P
H J E G K R H E S N O S I R P
T Q O A N H G W K A D O R E H
E B O H T A I J A M E S O F O
L E X D N H L X J Z N K A S M
```

by Ruth Graether

99

The Good Samaritan

Luke 10:30–36

And Jesus answering said, A **certain man** went **down** from **Jerusalem** to **Jericho**, and fell **among thieves**, which **stripped** him of his **raiment**, and **wounded** him, and departed, leaving him **half dead**. And by chance there came down a certain **priest** that way: and when he saw him, he passed by on the **other side**. And likewise a **Levite**, when he was at the **place**, came and **looked** on him, and **passed** by on the other side. But a certain **Samaritan**, as he **journeyed**, came where he was: and when he **saw** him, he had **compassion** on him, and went to him, and **bound** up his **wounds**, **pouring** in **oil** and **wine**, and set him on his own **beast**, and brought him to an **inn**, and **took care** of him. And on the **morrow** when he **departed**, he took out **two pence**, and **gave** them to the **host**, and said unto him, Take care of him; and whatsoever thou spendest **more**, when I come again, I **will repay** thee. Which now of these three, thinkest thou, was neighbour unto him that fell among the thieves?

```
D E Y E N R O U J E R I C H O
M K O O T H E R R A I M E N T
M S T R I P P E D I S P P S G
D O C E R T A I N E R A C A N
E C R W O U N D E D E R O M I
P C O R Z P M A D M C D S A R
A A N M O Y A P E R A N D R U
R T N E P W N L S X L U N I O
T S I I P A A H S L P O U T P
E E E H V S S O A L O B O A L
D I J V U B G S P I E O W N L
E R J R E N E T I D F V K K I
N P E A O I L V O O E L I E W
I J S M B S H S A W N A A T D
W T A D O W N T H G T C D H E
```

by N. Teri Grottke

What was the first question of God's
recorded in the Bible?

God's question to Adam, "Where art thou?" (Genesis 3:9)

100 ___

Mary's Magnificat

Luke 1:46–55

And **Mary** said, My **soul** doth **magnify** the **Lord**, and my **spirit** hath **rejoiced** in **God** my **Saviour**. For he hath regarded the **low** estate of his handmaiden: for, behold, from henceforth all generations shall call me blessed. For he that is mighty hath done to me great **things**; and **holy** is his **name**. And his **mercy** is on them that **fear** him from generation to generation. He hath **shewed** strength with his **arm**; he hath **scattered** the **proud** in the imagination of their **hearts**. He hath put down the mighty from their **seats**, and **exalted** them of low **degree**. He hath **filled** the **hungry** with **good** things; and the **rich** he hath sent empty away. He hath **helped** his **servant Israel**, in **remembrance** of his mercy; as he **spake** to our fathers, to Abraham, and to his seed for ever.

```
R E D T R U O I V A S G D F D
E X T V N A R M S E H H R I E
M A N R A A O D Y G T O O L P
E L E M E R V T E G N N L L L
M T S S Q J P R N G Z I R E E
B E F E H M O R E S R L H D H
R D M Y E E T I P S O E U T D
A A L R F S W I C W T O E E K
N S U G O D R E G E R R R F P
C P O N Z I H O D P D E A A R
E A S U T I O J D M T S Q E K
I K H H G D L T R T E R M Y H
U E M A W A Y Q A A A R I C H
M A G N I F Y C T E G D C G I
I S R A E L S S F M A R Y A
```

by N. Teri Grottke

⚡Bonus Trivia

To what did James liken a tongue out of control?

Fire. (James 3:6)

101

The Pharisee and the Publican

Luke 18:10–14

Two men went up into the temple to **pray;** the one a Pharisee, and the **other** a **publican.** The **Pharisee stood** and **prayed thus** with **himself,** God, I **thank** thee, that I am not as other men are, extortioners, **unjust, adulterers,** or even as this publican. I **fast twice** in the **week,** I **give tithes** of **all** that I **possess.** And the publican, **standing afar off,** would not **lift** up so **much** as his **eyes** unto **heaven,** but **smote** upon his **breast, saying, God** be **merciful** to me a sinner. I **tell** you, this man went **down** to his **house** justified **rather** than the other: for **every one** that exalteth himself shall be **abased;** and he that **humbleth** himself shall be exalted.

```
B R E A S T F I L T S A F O M
Q D L K K N A H T G S F H F E
S S E S S O P Q N E F E U L N
A E G T W I C E H O V E M E W
W H O U S E V T L E P S B S L
E R D O E A I P R G R I L M U
D A W N E T E Y E S A R E I F
O T O H A B A S E D Y A T H I
O H T N A C I L B U P H H A C
T E J N O M U C H Y N P G T R
S R E R E T L U D A X J D H E
A A F A R W H I U G A O U U M
P R A Y E D B E I T W L Z S P
X F E T O M S V R N R L L E T
S A Y I N G E S T A N D I N G
```

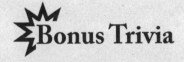

by N. Teri Grottke

Answers

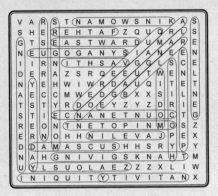

PUZZLE 1

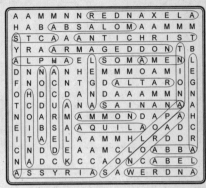

PUZZLE 2

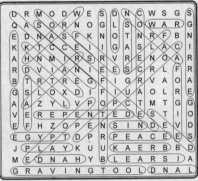

PUZZLE 3

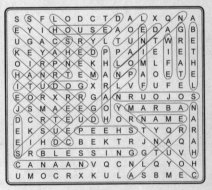

PUZZLE 4

PUZZLE 5

PUZZLE 6

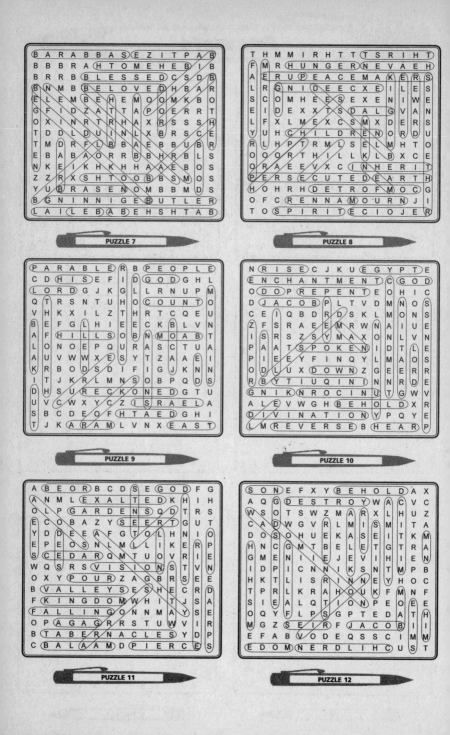

PUZZLE 7

PUZZLE 8

PUZZLE 9

PUZZLE 10

PUZZLE 11

PUZZLE 12

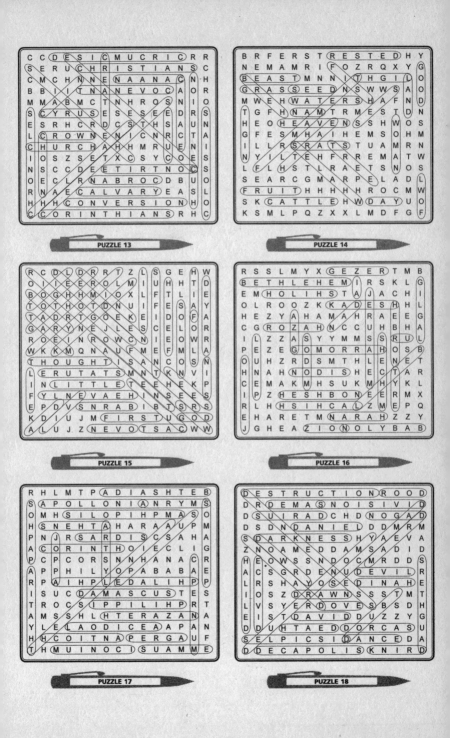

PUZZLE 13

PUZZLE 14

PUZZLE 15

PUZZLE 16

PUZZLE 17

PUZZLE 18

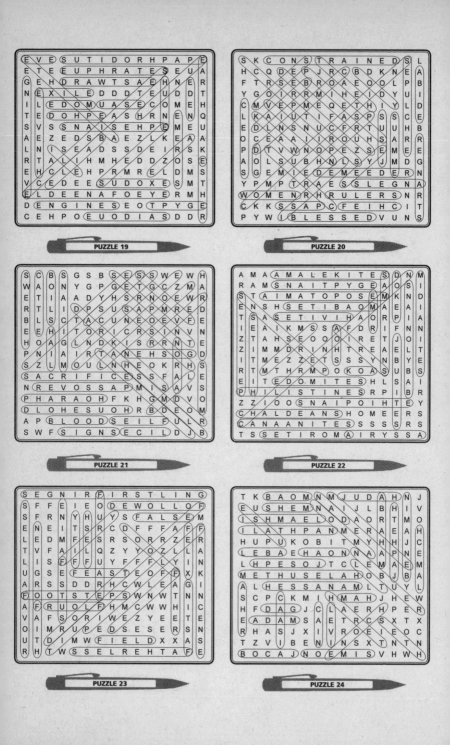

PUZZLE 19

PUZZLE 20

PUZZLE 21

PUZZLE 22

PUZZLE 23

PUZZLE 24

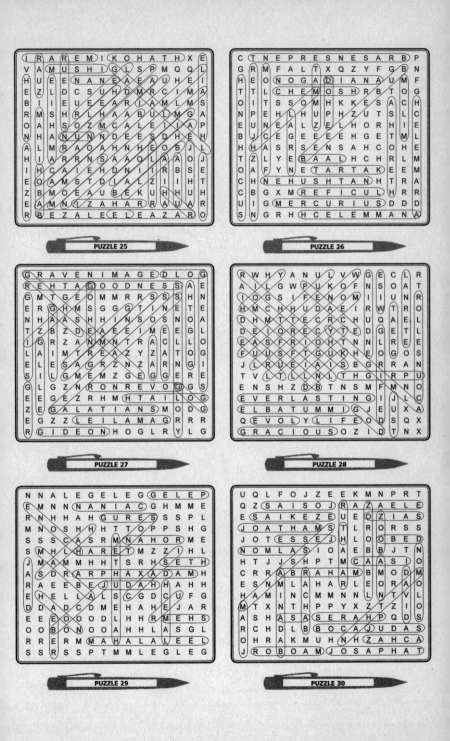

PUZZLE 25

PUZZLE 26

PUZZLE 27

PUZZLE 28

PUZZLE 29

PUZZLE 30

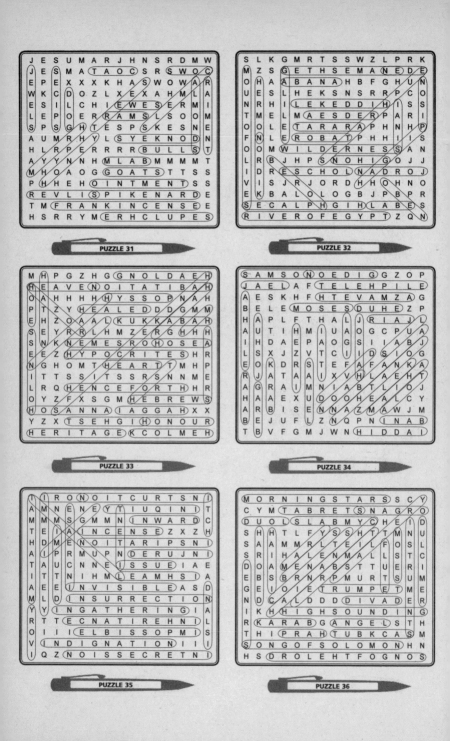

PUZZLE 31

PUZZLE 32

PUZZLE 33

PUZZLE 34

PUZZLE 35

PUZZLE 36

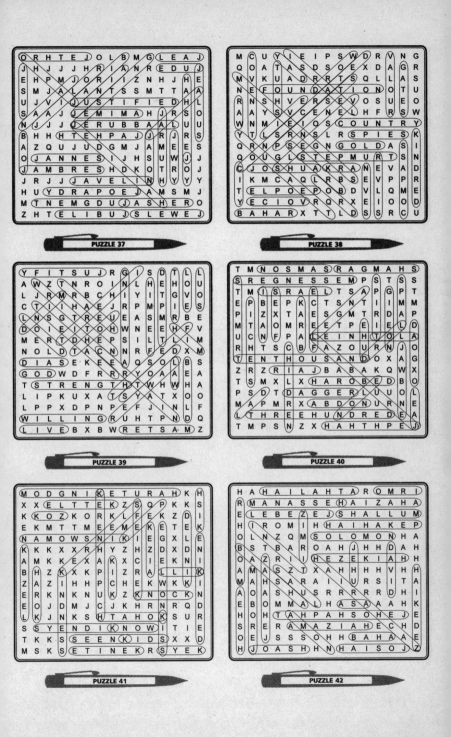

PUZZLE 37

PUZZLE 38

PUZZLE 39

PUZZLE 40

PUZZLE 41

PUZZLE 42

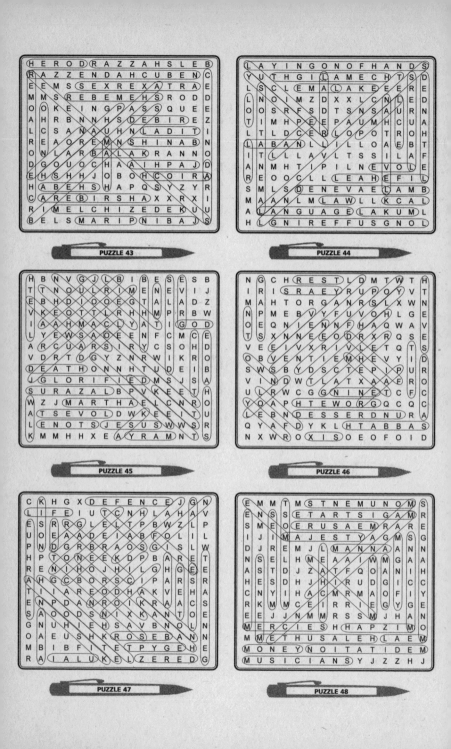

PUZZLE 43

PUZZLE 44

PUZZLE 45

PUZZLE 46

PUZZLE 47

PUZZLE 48

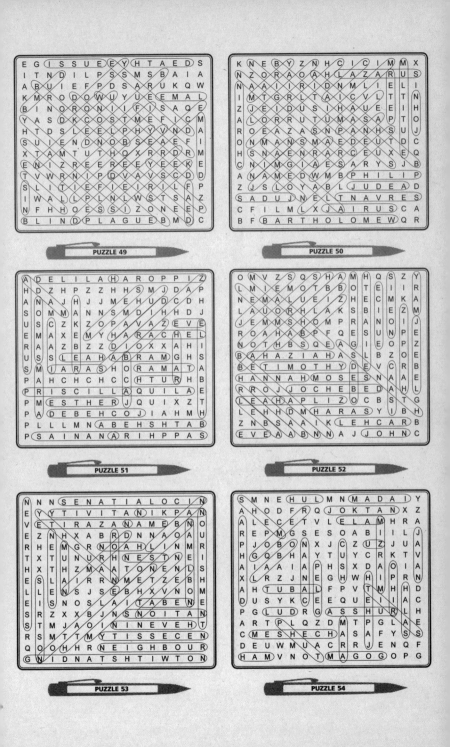

PUZZLE 49

PUZZLE 50

PUZZLE 51

PUZZLE 52

PUZZLE 53

PUZZLE 54

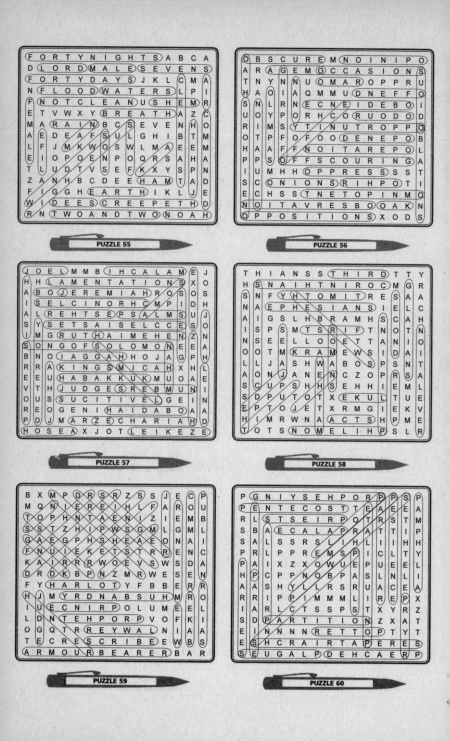

PUZZLE 55

PUZZLE 56

PUZZLE 57

PUZZLE 58

PUZZLE 59

PUZZLE 60

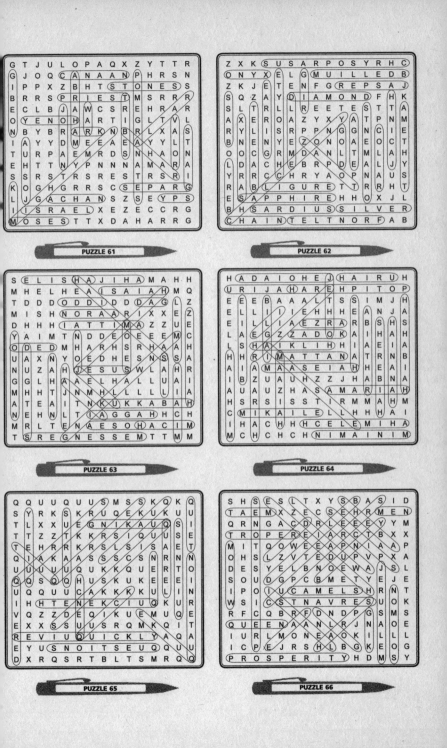

PUZZLE 61

PUZZLE 62

PUZZLE 63

PUZZLE 64

PUZZLE 65

PUZZLE 66

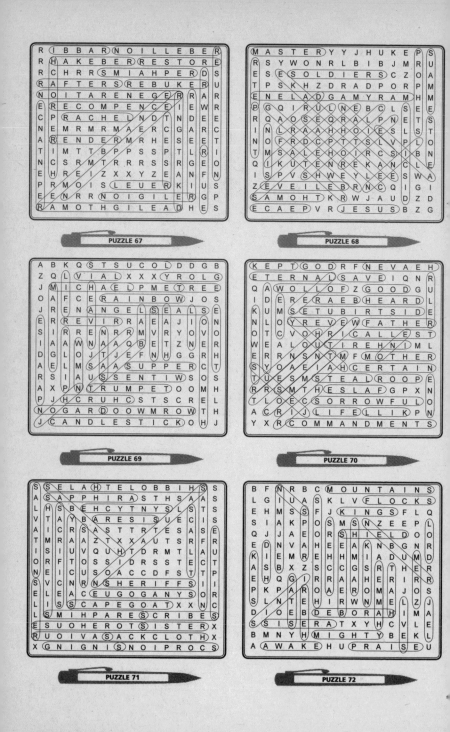

PUZZLE 67

PUZZLE 68

PUZZLE 69

PUZZLE 70

PUZZLE 71

PUZZLE 72

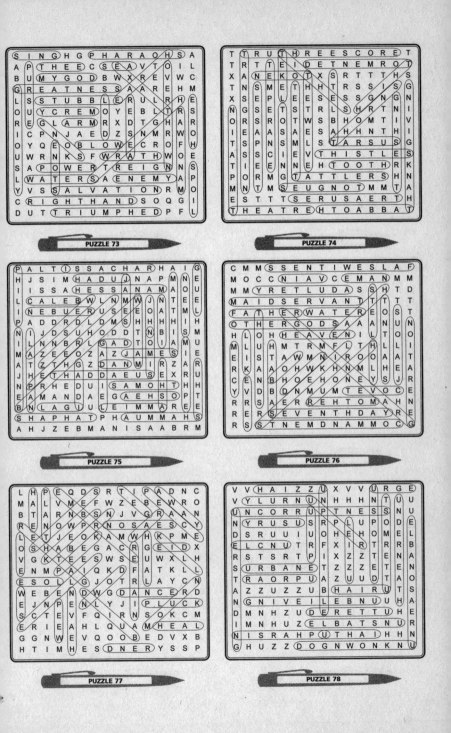

PUZZLE 73

PUZZLE 74

PUZZLE 75

PUZZLE 76

PUZZLE 77

PUZZLE 78

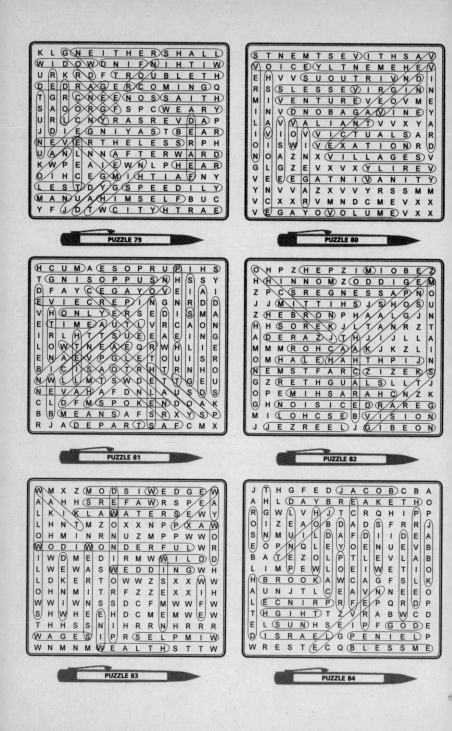

PUZZLE 79

PUZZLE 80

PUZZLE 81

PUZZLE 82

PUZZLE 83

PUZZLE 84

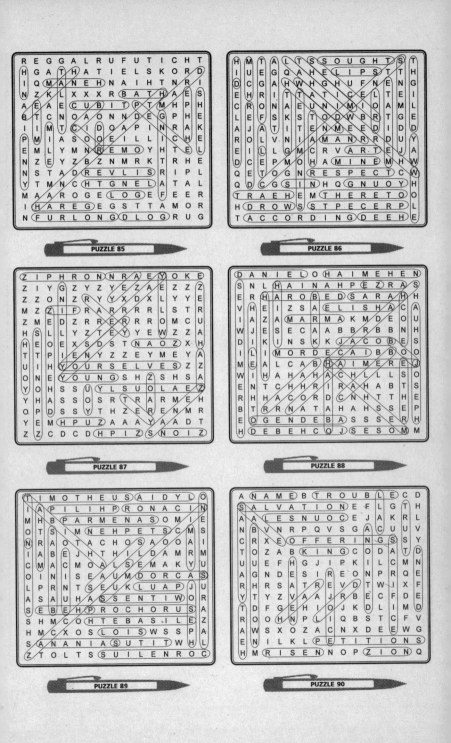

PUZZLE 85

PUZZLE 86

PUZZLE 87

PUZZLE 88

PUZZLE 89

PUZZLE 90

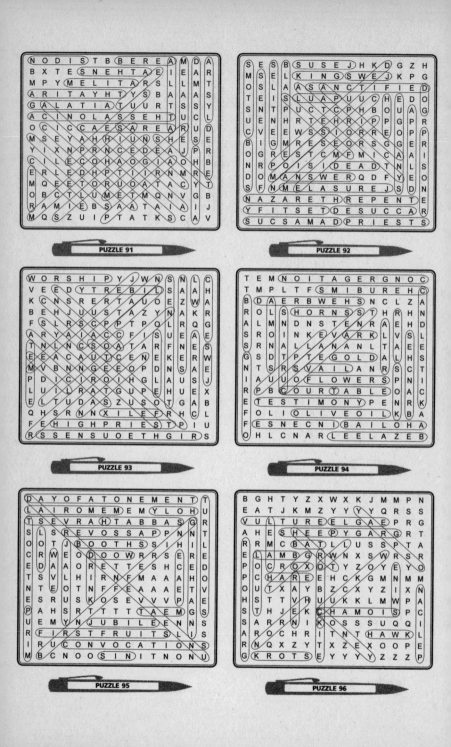

PUZZLE 91

PUZZLE 92

PUZZLE 93

PUZZLE 94

PUZZLE 95

PUZZLE 96

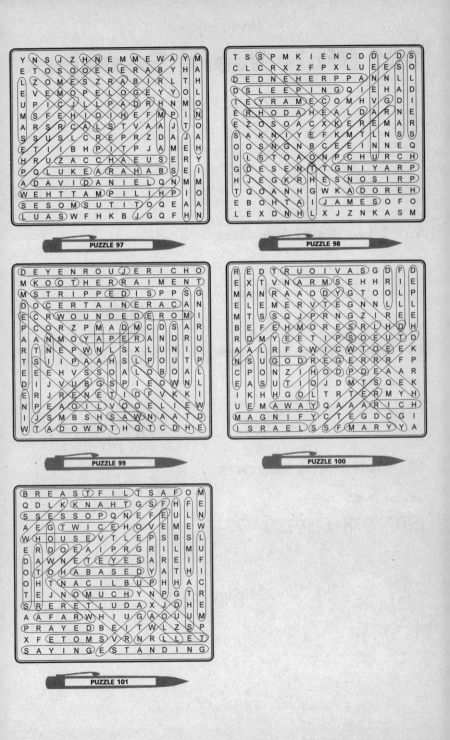

PUZZLE 97

PUZZLE 98

PUZZLE 99

PUZZLE 100

PUZZLE 101

If you enjoyed

101 Bible Word Searches

VOLUME 1

~check out these titles for hours of fun!

101 Bible Word Searches

VOLUME 2

ISBN 978-1-59789-475-3

101 Bible Word Searches

VOLUME 3

ISBN 978-1-59789-476-0

101 Bible Word Searches

VOLUME 4

ISBN 978-1-59789-477-7

224 pages each.